MW01074217

LINUX COMMANDS BY EXAMPLE

KHALED JAMAL

Copyright © 2018 Khaled Jamal

All rights reserved.

ISBN: 9781980761747

FORWARD

This book is intended for IT fellows who want to acquire a basic to inter-mediate Linux knowledge rapidly.

I used many references to arrange it in such a way to be clear, extremely focused and practical.

The key of getting full benefit is to install the nice tool in the first chapter, to read and execute the examples, by the end of this practice you will be able to use commands and deal comfortably with Linux.

CONTENTS

1 GETTING STARTED

This chapter provides general information about the Linux file system, explains what a distribution is and finally shows you how to prepare a light environment to practice commands.

The root

In a file system, there is always what is called a root, which is a big base folder that contains all the other folders and files.

Windows has actually several roots. C:\ is the root of your hard drive; D:\ could be the root of your CD drive.

Linux has one root that is the slash "/". There is no higher level folder than "/".

The directory contents

We'll make you here a list of the most common directories found directly under Linux root "/".

It is important to get an idea about it, but don't worry if you don't **fully** understand the meaning of each of these directories.

/bin: contains programs (executable) that can be used by all users of the machine.

/boot: contains files for booting Linux.

/dev: contains subfolders that represent each device. For example, there are files that represent your partitions and CD drive.

/etc: contains configuration files specific to the system.

/home: contains by default the user home directories, each user of the computer has his personal folder in here. For example, my personal home directory is /home/Khaled Jamal.

/lib: contains the shared libraries used by the programs.

/media: when a removable device (such as an SD memory card or a USB flash drive) is inserted into your computer, Linux allows you to access it from a subfolder of /media.

/proc: contains information about the system state and processes.

/root: this is the root user's home directory, normally, the personal folders are placed in home, but that of "root" is an exception. Because "root" is the super user, he is entitled to a special space.

/usr: this is one of the biggest files, in which will settle most of the programs requested by the user.

/tmp: contains temporary files created by programs during system use.

/var: contains "variable" data, often logs (written traces of what has happened recently on the computer).

Linux distributions

The Linux operating system isn't produced by a single organization. Different organizations and people work on different parts, for example there's:

The Linux kernel: the core of the operating system.

The GNU shell utilities: the terminal interface and many of the commands you use.

The X server: produces a graphical desktop.

The desktop environment: runs on the X server to provide a graphical desktop.

And more, System services, graphical programs, many are developed independently from another. They're all open-source software distributed in source code form.

Linux distributions take all the code from the open-source projects and compile it for you, combining it into a single operating system you can boot up and install. They also make choices for you, such as choosing the default desktop environment, browser, and other software. Most distributions add their own finishing touches, such as themes and custom software.

There are multiple different Linux distributions, if you're a desktop user, you'll probably want something simple, like Ubuntu or Mint. Others are suited for different purposes like Red Hat, Centos, Fedora, and OpenSuse.

Cygwin

Cygwin is a large collection of Open Source tools which provide functionality similar to a Linux distribution on Windows.

I recommend using this light tool to practice the examples, later when you become familiar with the subject we'll set up a more advanced environment.

To install Cygwin, open this link http://cygwin.com/ in your web browser, then Look for the setup-x86.exe (32-bit installation) or setup-x86_64.exe (64-bit installation) link and click on it to download the appropriate setup program.

The installation is straightforward, run the Cygwin setup program, keep the default configuration and click next many times till you come at the screen for selecting the packages.

By default, the executable will install only the packages in the Base category and their dependencies, resulting in a minimal Cygwin installation and that is sufficient for our purpose.

Just keep the default and click next, the base packages will be download-ed and installed automatically.

Finally check the Create icon on Desktop and click finish to close the set-up program.

Go to your Desktop and click on the Cygwin icon, the console will show up:

Type whoami to print the user id.

Click on the icon in the upper left corner and choose Options, there you can customize all kinds of things, the foreground and the background, the font, the cursor …

2 MAN PAGES

The manual pages are a set of pages that explain every command available on your system including what they do, the specifics of how you run
them and what command line arguments they accept.

The man command is very easy to use, it takes as parameter the name of
the command whose doc you want to read.

man mkdir

Type the following command: (to quit the manual press q)

```
$ man mkdir
```

Your console should display something like this:

```
NAME
        mkdir - make directories
SYNOPSIS
        mkdir [OPTION]... DIRECTORY...
DESCRIPTION
        Create the DIRECTORY(ies), if they do not already exist.


Mandatory arguments to long options are mandatory for short op-
tions too.
```

```
     -m, --mode=MODE

           set file mode (as in chmod), not a=rwx - umask

     -p, --parents

           no error if existing, make parent directories as
needed

......
```

Let's explain the most important section which is the SYNOPSIS:

```
mkdir [OPTION]... DIRECTORY...
```

[OPTION]: after mkdir, you can write an option. We put square brackets to indicate that it is optional. You don't have to write an option.

DIRECTORY: it is the name of the directory to create. This parameter is mandatory since it is not in square brackets.

...: the term DIRECTORY is followed by suspension points. This means that we can repeat DIRECTORY as many times as we want. It means we can specify several directories to create at once.

Obviously [OPTION]... means we can specify as many options as we want.

SYNOPSIS words written in bold are words to type as they are. Underlined words must be replaced by the appropriate name, this is logical, we must write precisely mkdir, however we should not write DIRECTORY but the name of the directory to create.

All options in the description section can be used instead of [OPTION] in the SYNOPSIS.

man cp

Let's try a slightly more complex command: cp. It is used to copy files and directories.

Type the following command:

```
$ man cp
```

Your console displays this synopsis:

```
SYNOPSIS

      cp [OPTION]... [-T] SOURCE DEST

      cp [OPTION]... SOURCE... DIRECTORY

      cp [OPTION]... -t DIRECTORY SOURCE...

...
```

Here is the explanation of each part:

cp [OPTION] ... [-T] SOURCE DEST : The only thing required here are the parameters SOURCE (the name of the file to copy) and DEST (the name of the copy to be created) .These files can be preceded by one or more options (note the ellipsis) as well as the -T option.

cp [OPTION]... SOURCE... DIRECTORY: This time you can copy one or more files (SOURCE...) to a directory (DIRECTORY). All of this can again be preceded by one or more options.

cp [OPTION]... -t DIRECTORY SOURCE... : This means that we can also write the directory (DIRECTORY) at first, followed by one or more files (SOURCE...). Be careful, in this case it is mandatory to use the -t parameter which is no longer in square brackets.

man file

The file command is used to determine file type.

Type this command:

```
$ man file
```

Your console displays:

```
SYNOPSIS

file [-bcdEhiklLNnprsvzZ0] [--apple] [--extension] [--mime-
encoding] [--mime-type][-e testname] [-F separator] [-f namefile]
[-m magicfiles] [-P name=value] file ...

...
```

The file command must begin with "file" (this word is written in bold). That's logical.

Then you can use one of the options -bcdEh... (you can use -b, but also -bc, -d, -dEs, -dcdEh ...). These options are in square brackets, so they are optional.

Same then for other options which are optional. However, you will notice that -e for example must be followed by a value.

The fact that testname, separator or namefile are underlined means that you don't have to copy these words as they are in the console: you have to replace them with a suitable value.

Options section

This section describes all of the options from the synopsis.

Type this command:

```
$ man rm
```

Your console displays:

```
NAME
        rm - remove files or directories

SYNOPSIS
        rm [OPTION]... [FILE]...

DESCRIPTION
        This manual page documents the GNU version of rm.  rm re-
moves each specified file.  By default, it does not remove direc-
tories.

        ...

OPTIONS

        ...

        -i      prompt before every removal

        ...

        -r, -R, --recursive
                remove directories and their contents recursively

        -d, --dir
```

```
        remove empty directories
...
```

The name and description sections describe what the command does, and if you look at the -r option, they say it removes directories and their contents recursively. The other options in the same line (-R and --recursive) do the same thing, so you can write:

```
$ rm -r xdirectory
```

Or

```
$ rm -R xdirectory
```

Or

```
$ rm --recursive xdirectory
```

man -k or apropos

The -k option is used to search the man pages for a command. Suppose you want to get information about your disk space usage, type the following command:

```
$ man -k disk space
```

It would list all the commands with disk (and or) space in the command **name or description**.

You can search the exact expression by adding quotes: (this command doesn't work on Cygwin but would return a result on a real Linux system)

```
$ man -k 'disk space'
df (1)                  - report file system disk space usage
```

The same could be achieved using apropos:

```
$ apropos 'disk space'
df (1)                  - report file system disk space usage
```

Notice the df command that reports file system disk space usage.

df --help

Now that you've found the df command, let's get some help, you can use the man df command to view the complete documentation, but we'll use the --help option to get less details and quick help:

```
$ df --help
Usage: df [OPTION]... [FILE]...

Show information about the file system on which each FILE re-
sides,

or all file systems by default.

...

...

  -h, --human-readable  print sizes in human readable format
(e.g., 1K

 234M 2G)

...
```

By using the help, you can type this command to get information about all file systems:

```
$ df -h
Filesystem       Size  Used Avail Use% Mounted on
C:/cygwin2       288G  172G  117G  60% /
```

Or this command to get information about the file system on which **/etc** resides:

```
$ df -h /etc
Filesystem       Size  Used Avail Use% Mounted on
C:/cygwin2       288G  172G  117G  60% /
```

Note: the result would be different on a real Linux machine where several file systems exist (e.g. more than one partition or volume).

Searching

It is possible to search within a manual page. To do this, while you're in a particular manual page, press forward slash '/' followed by the word you look for and hit 'Enter'.

If the word appears multiple times you may cycle through by pressing the 'n' for next or 'N' for precedent.

Type the following command:

```
$ man df
```

Search for the word 'space' (/space), press Enter and navigate over the search result using 'n' o 'N'.

3 WORKING WITH DIRECTORIES

In this chapter, we'll learn how to navigate through directories and list their contents.

pwd

The pwd command (Print Working Directory) displays your current directory:

```
$ pwd
/home/Khaled Jamal
```

cd

The cd command (Change Directory) is used to change the current directory:

```
$ cd /etc
$ pwd
/etc


$cd /bin
$pwd
/bin
```

Just typing cd without a target directory, will get you back into your home directory:

```
$cd /bin

$pwd

/bin


$cd

$pwd

/home/Khaled Jamal
```

To go up to the direct parent directory use cd followed by a double dot(..):

```
$pwd

/home/Khaled Jamal


$cd ..

$pwd

/home


$cd ..

$pwd

/
```

You can use the double dot(..) several times to get to n parent in one shot like this:

```
$ cd


$ pwd

/home/Khaled Jamal


$ cd ../..
```

```
$ pwd
/
```

Absolute and relative paths

When you type a path starting with **slash (/)**, then you're using an absolute path beginning from the root.

Remember, Linux has one root that is **the slash (/).**

From anywhere in the directory tree, you can use an absolute path to get exactly where you want:

```
$pwd
/home/Khaled Jamal

$cd /usr/bin

$pwd
/usr/bin
```

Let's start from the root:

```
$cd /

$ls
bin   cygdrive  Cygwin.bat  Cygwin.ico  Cygwin-Terminal.ico  dev
etc   home  lib  proc  sbin  tmp  usr  var

$pwd
/
```

Now if you type cd etc, the system assumes the current directory (slash /) as a starting point, which means it puts you in /etc:

```
$cd etc
```

```
$pwd
/etc
```

That's what we call a relative path. It's a path relative to the current working directory.

Tab completion

This mechanism is very helpful to speed up typing commands, it is case sensitive and can be used while typing **commands, options or file names.**

For example, typing cd /ho followed by the tab key will expand the command line to cd /home/.

The same thing can be applied to commands, you should just enter enough letters followed by the tab key and the terminal would guess what you want to type.

ls

The ls command is used for listing the content of a directory:

```
$cd /

$ls
bin   cygdrive  Cygwin.bat  Cygwin.ico  Cygwin-Terminal.ico  dev
etc   home  lib   proc  sbin  tmp   usr   var
```

ls -a

We use ls with -a (all) option to show all files and directories including hidden files.

Hidden files start with a dot and don't show up in regular file listings.

Type cd to go back to your home directory, then try ls -a command:

```
$ cd
```

```
$ pwd
/home/Khaled Jamal


$ ls -a
.    .bash_history  .bashrc    .lesshst    .profile
.shell-script.sh.swo
..   .bash_profile  .inputrc  .minttyrc  .shell-script.sh.swn
.shell-script.sh.swp
```

ls -l

The l letter means long listing format, it gives more details for each file such as, size, permissions, owners, dates etc:

```
$cd /


$ls -l
total 309
drwxr-xr-x+     1 ...         0 15 Oct.  00:49 bin
dr-xr-xr-x      1 ...         0 15 Oct.  02:09 cygdrive
-rwxr-xr-x      1 ...        57 20 Jul. 20:12 Cygwin.bat
-rw-r--r--      1 ... 157097 20 Jul. 20:12 Cygwin.ico
...
```

ls -lh

The -h option shows the file sizes in more human readable format, so instead of 157097 in the last example, it shows 154K:

```
$cd /


$ls -lh
total 309
drwxr-xr-x+     1 ...         0 15 Oct. 00:49 bin
```

```
dr-xr-xr-x        1 …          0 15 Oct. 02:09 cygdrive

-rwxr-xr-x        1 …         57 20 Jul. 20:12 Cygwin.bat

-rw-r--r--        1 …       157K 20 Jul. 20:12 Cygwin.ico

…
```

There are many ways to combine these options, ls -hl or ls -l -h or ls -h -l all give the same result.

ls -F

The -F option append an indicator that distinguishes for example a file from a directory:

```
$cd /

$ls -lhF
total 309
drwxr-xr-x+       1 …          0 15 Oct. 00:49 bin/

dr-xr-xr-x        1 …          0 15 Oct. 02:09 cygdrive/

-rwxr-xr-x        1 …         57 20 Jul. 20:12 Cygwin.bat*

-rw-r--r--        1 …       157K 20 Jul. 20:12 Cygwin.ico

…
```

Entries with a slash suffix are directories (bin/, cygdrive/), here are the different indicators:

/ is a directory.

@ is a symbolic link.

| is a named pipe.

= is a socket.

* for executable files.

ls -lt

The -t option sorts entries by modification time, the newest displays the first:

```
$ ls -lt /
total 313
dr-xr-xr-x  1 … 0 Dec. 18 00:46 cygdrive
dr-xr-xr-x  9 … 0 Dec. 18 00:46 proc
drwxrwxrwt+ 1 … 0 Dec. 13 23:59 tmp
drwxr-xr-x+ 1 … 0 Nov.  5 15:44 desktop
drwxr-xr-x+ 1 … 0 Nov.  2 21:12 etc
drwxrwxrwt+ 1 … 0 Nov.  1 21:37 home
...
```

ls -lrt

The -rt option is used to reverse order while sorting, suppose you have a long list to display and you want to bring the newest modified files at last (to avoid scrolling up), you'll need the -rt options:

```
$ ls -lrt /
total 313
...
-rwxr-xr-x  1 … 58 Nov.  1 21:37 Cygwin.bat
drwxrwxrwt+ 1 …  0 Nov.  1 21:37 home
drwxr-xr-x+ 1 …  0 Nov.  2 21:12 etc
drwxr-xr-x+ 1 …  0 Nov.  5 15:44 desktop
drwxrwxrwt+ 1 …  0 Dec. 13 23:59 tmp
dr-xr-xr-x  9 …  0 Dec. 18 00:54 proc
dr-xr-xr-x  1 …  0 Dec. 18 00:54 cygdrive
```

mkdir

The mkdir (make directories) command creates one or more directories if they don't exist:

```
$ cd

$ mkdir document movies projects

$ ls -lh
total 1.0K

drwxr-xr-x+ 1 … 0 Jan. 16 17:41 document
drwxr-xr-x+ 1 … 0 Jan. 16 17:41 movies
drwxr-xr-x+ 1 … 0 Jan. 16 17:41 projects
```

The tilde ~

The tilde is used to refer to the current user's home directory which is normally at /home/username.

For example, below we're going to /etc, then to 'document' on the current user's home directory using the tilde:

```
$ echo ~
/home/Khaled Jamal

$ cd /etc

$ cd ~/document/

$ pwd
/home/Khaled Jamal/document
```

4 WORKING WITH FILES

In Linux world everything is a file, even a directory is a special kind of files, each partition or process, **everything** is represented as a file, and files are **case sensitive,** which means a file named 'host' is different from another named 'Host'.

file

The file command determines file type.

The following command returns the file types of all files under /etc:

```
$ file /etc/*
/etc/alternatives:      directory
/etc/bash.bash_logout:  ASCII text
/etc/bash.bashrc:       ASCII text
/etc/defaults:          directory
/etc/fstab.d:           sticky, directory
/etc/hosts:             symbolic link to
/cygdrive/c/Windows/System32/drivers/etc/hosts
…
```

Note: The star '*' represents zero or more characters, we'll come to wild-cards in a later chapter.

touch

The touch command creates empty files:

```
$ cd
$pwd
/home/Khaled Jamal

$touch notes.txt
$ls -lh
total 0
-rw-r--r-- 1 … 0 15 Oct.   16:12 notes.txt
```

rm

The rm command removes files or directories forever:

```
$rm notes.txt
$ls -lh
total0
```

rm -i

Use rm command along with the -i option to prevent yourself from accidentally removing a file:

```
$touch notes.txt
$ls -lh
total 0
-rw-r--r-- 1 … 0 15 Oct.   16:12 notes.txt

$rm -i notes.txt
rm: remove regular empty file `notes.txt? yes
$ls -lh
total0
```

rm -rf

The rm -rf (-recursive -force) command is used to remove directories and all their contents recursively.

Let's create this structure 'folder/subfolder/', mkdir -p is a fast way to do it:

```
$ cd
$pwd
/home/Khaled Jamal


$mkdir -p folder/subfolder
```

Then we create a file inside that structure:

```
$touch folder/subfolder/notes.txt
```

And we use ls -R command to list subdirectories recursively:

```
$pwd
/home/Khaled Jamal
$ls –R

.:
folder


./folder:
subfolder


./folder/subfolder:
notes.txt
```

Note: The dot (./folder) simply means the current directory.

Finally we erase the folder and all its contents using rm -rf:

```
$rm -rf folder
```

```
$ls -lhF

   total 0
```

cp

To copy a file, use **cp** with a source and a target arguments.

Let's create a file named notes.txt and copy it to another newly created file named notescopy.txt:

```
$pwd
/home/Khaled Jamal


$touch notes.txt


$ cp notes.txt notescopy.txt


$ ls -lh
total 0
-rw-r--r-- 1 … 0 Jan. 16 21:13 notes.txt
-rw-r--r-- 1 … 0 Jan. 16 21:14 notescopy.txt
```

After that we create a directory named folder and we copy those files to it:

```
$mkdir folder


$cp notes.txt notescopy.txt folder/


$ ls -lh folder
total 0
-rw-r--r-- 1 … 0 17 Oct.  22:18 notes.txt
-rw-r--r-- 1 … 0 17 Oct.  22:18 notescopy.txt
```

cp -r

To copy directories and all files in all subdirectories, use **cp -r** (recursive).

We do that and copy our 'folder' directory to the /tmp directory:

```
$ cp -r folder /tmp


$ ls -R /tmp
/tmp:
folder


/tmp/folder:
notes.txt   notescopy.txt
```

mv

If the source and the destination are both files, then mv is used for re-naming.

Let's rename the notescopy.txt file to backup.txt:

```
$ ls
folder   notes.txt   notescopy.txt


$ mv notescopy.txt backup.txt


$ ls
backup.txt   folder   notes.txt
```

The same thing applies to directories; try to rename 'folder' to 'documents':

```
$ ls
backup.txt   folder   notes.txt
```

```
$ mv folder documents


$ ls

backup.txt   documents   notes.txt
```

What about moving all txt files to the documents directory?

```
$ ls

backup.txt   documents   notes.txt


$ mv backup.txt notes.txt documents/


$ ls documents

backup.txt   notes.txt   notescopy.txt
```

Use mv also to move a directory to another existing directory.

In the following example we move the 'documents' directory to the /tmp directory:

```
$ pwd
/home/Khaled Jamal


$ ls
documents


$ mv documents /tmp


$ ls /tmp
documents   folder
```

basename

When you provide a string that contains a file name will full path, base-name will remove only the directory portion of it, and return the file name portion of that string.

Here is an example where we extract file and directory names using the basename command :

```
$ basename /etc/profile
profile


$ basename /etc/profile.d
profile.d
```

To get only the filename without the extension, you should pass the extension as a second argument to the basename command as shown below :

```
$ basename /etc/man_db.conf .conf
man_db
```

This command is very useful when the argument is a variable that changes according to a bash script processing, here is an idea about it:

```
$ usr_bin_path=/usr/bin/cmp.exe
$ basename $usr_bin_path
cmp.exe
```

Note: we'll learn bash scripting in a later chapter.

5 WORKING WITH FILE CONTENTS

In this chapter we'll learn how to display text file contents with head, tail, cat, more, and less commands.

head

The head command is used to output the first part of files.

In the following example we display the first ten lines of /etc/profile:

```
$ pwd
/home/Khaled Jamal


$ cd /etc


$ head profile
# To the extent possible under law, the author(s) have …
# copyright and related and neighboring rights to this …
…
```

You can easily display as much lines as you want by specifying a number option:

```
$ head -2 profile
# To the extent possible under law, the author(s) …
```

```
# copyright and related and neighboring rights to ...
```

tail

Likewise you can use the tail command to display the last part of files.

Let's show the last two lines of /etc/bash.bashrc:

```
$ tail -2 /etc/bash.bashrc
# Uncomment to use the terminal colours set in DIR_COLORS
# eval "$(dircolors -b /etc/DIR_COLORS)"
```

cat

The cat (short for "concatenate") is used to view contents of one or multiple files on the screen.

Let's create two files using echo and ">>" commands, then make use of cat to display contents:

```
$ echo 'This is demo1' >> demo1.txt
$ echo 'This is demo2' >> demo2.txt


$ ls
demo1.txt   demo2.txt


$ cat demo1.txt
This is demo1


$ cat demo2.txt
This is demo2
```

The cat command is used also to concatenate files into bigger files:

```
$ cat demo1.txt demo2.txt > demos.txt


$ ls
```

```
demo1.txt demo2.txt demos.txt


$ cat demos.txt

This is demo1

This is demo2
```

cat is used evenly to create text files.

Type cat > text-file.txt, press enter then type one or more lines, finishing each line with the enter key. After the last line, press enter then press Ctr+d:

```
$ cat > text-file.txt

This is the first line

This is the second line


$ ls -l

total 4

-rw-r--r-- 1 … 14  1 Nov.   21:46 demo1.txt

-rw-r--r-- 1 … 14  1 Nov.   21:46 demo2.txt

-rw-r--r-- 1 … 28  2 Nov.   20:50 demos.txt

-rw-r--r-- 1 … 47  2 Nov.   21:03 text-file.txt
```

more

The more command is used to display file content that take up more than one screen.

Type the following command to display the /etc/profile content:

```
$ more /etc/profile

# To the extent possible under law, the author(s) have …

…

…

…
```

```
---Plus--(29%)
```

In order to navigate through the file line by line press Enter key, or press Spacebar key to navigate one page at a time, the page being your current terminal screen size.

To exit the command, **press q key**.

A useful option of the more command is the -number switch which allows you to set the number of line a page should contain, type the following command and navigate through the file:

```
$ more -10 /etc/profile
```

The more command can be used also with pipes in a multitude of Linux commands in order to narrow their screen output allowing you to scroll through results.

To understand this, type the following command and look what it returns:

```
$ ls -l /usr/bin | more -10
```

The command (ls -l /usr/bin) displays the list of files under /usr/bin.

The pipe (|) feeds the output from the program on the left (ls -l /usr/bin) as input to the program on the right (more -10).

The command (more -10) displays ten lines of the piped input.

less

Similar to more, less command allows you to view the content of a file and navigate through it. The main difference between more and less is that less command is faster and allows navigation using up/down keys and other keys.

Type the same command as before with less:

```
$ less /etc/profile
```

Navigate through the file by pressing Enter, Spacebar, up/down keys, **G** to move to the last line of the file, **1G** to move to the first line of the file.

In order to display a file starting at a specific line number, use the following syntax:

```
$ less +10 /etc/profile
```

If you need to track down the number of every line with the less command, use the -N option like this:

```
$ less -N /etc/profile
1 # To the extent possible under law, the author(s) …
2 # copyright and related and neighboring rights to …
3 # public domain worldwide. This software is …
…
…
/etc/profile
```

To open a file at the first occurrence of a pattern, use the following syntax:

The pattern here is the word "shell".

```
less +/shell /etc/profile
# /etc/profile: executed by the command interpreter for login
shells.


# The latest version as installed by the Cygwin Setup program can
# always be found at /etc/defaults/etc/profile
…
…
```

A useful feature of this command is the use of **/word-to-search** option.

Type this command:

```
$ less /etc/profile
```

Then type /shell and press Enter to search the "shell" keyword, press n to repeat the search in a forward direction, or N to repeat it backward.

```
# To the extent possible under law, the author(s) have dedicated all

# copyright and related and neighboring rights to this software to the

…

…

/shell
```

6 IO REDIRECTION

Every program we run on the command line has three data streams connected to it.

STDIN (0) - Standard input: data fed into the program.

STDOUT (1) - Standard output: data printed by the program, defaults to the terminal.

STDERR (2) - Standard error: for error messages, also defaults to the terminal.

Piping and redirection are the means by which we may connect these streams between programs and files to direct data in interesting and useful ways.

Redirection

The greater than operator (>) indicates to the command line that we wish the programs output to be saved in a file instead of printed to the screen.

Let's see an example where we redirect the ls output to a file:

```
$ pwd
/home/Khaled Jamal

$ ls /etc > output.txt
```

```
$ cat output.txt
alternatives
bash.bash_logout
bash.bashrc
defaults
...
```

Note that the file is created first (if it does not already exist) and then the program is run, and output saved into the file.

If we save into a file which already exists, its content will be cleared, then the new output saved to it:

```
$ echo This is a test > output.txt
$ cat output.txt
This is a test
```

We can instead get the new data to be appended to the file using the double greater than operator (>>):

```
$ echo 'This line will be appended to the file' >> output.txt

$ cat output.txt
This is a test
This line will be appended to the file
```

The less than operator (<) sends data the other way. We read data from the file and feed it into the program via its STDIN stream.

For example, here we count the lines in the output.txt file:

```
$ wc -l < output.txt
2
```

We may easily combine the two forms of redirection we've seen so far into a single command.

In the following example we look for lines with the word 'appended' in the output.txt file, and then put the result in another newly created file:

```
$ grep 'appended' < output.txt > grep-result.txt


$ cat grep-result.txt
This line will be appended to the file
```

Note: grep is a search command, we'll talk about it later.

Now let's look at the third stream which is Standard Error or STDERR.

Before that we want to mention that these streams have numbers associated with them and we may use these numbers to identify the streams.

STDERR is stream number 2.

If we place a number before the greater (>) operator, then it will redirect that stream.

In the example below, we use the rm command to delete **two existing files**, but we include in the arguments, a file that does not exist, the rm command runs, and redirects errors to the errors.txt file:

```
$ rm grep-result.txt output.txt no-such-file.txt 2> errors.txt


$ ls
errors.txt


$ cat errors.txt
rm: cannot remove 'no-such-file.txt': No such file or directory
```

Piping

Piping is a mechanism for sending data from one program to another, the operator we use is (|). What this operator does is to feed the output from the program on the left as input to the program on the right.

In this example we list only the first three files in the /etc directory:

```
$ ls /etc | head -3
alternatives
bash.bash_logout
bash.bashrc
```

So the output of ls /etc is sent to the head command which prints only three lines from this output.

We may pipe as many programs together as we like. For example here we pipe the previous output to the tail command so as to get only the third file:

```
$ ls /etc | head -3 | tail -1
bash.bashrc
```

7 SHELL VARIABLES

An environment variable is a setting that the operating system, or programs working in the operating system access.

Shell variable

A shell variable is a variable that is available in **the current shell** (the current command line interpreter); it is only seen by built in shell commands.

In the following example, we create a shell variable and try to act on:

```
$ NAME=kevin
```

Below we display this variable's value by using built in shell commands like echo, printf or set:

```
$ echo $NAME
kevin


$ printf $NAME
kevin
```

Note: To read a variable's value, both $VARNAME or ${VARNAME} are valid forms to use.

set is a built in shell command that displays all variables in the system, let's use it and redirect its output to the grep command that searches and displays the NAME variable:

```
$ set | grep kevin
NAME=kevin
```

But this variable won't be seen by external commands like env.

env is not a built in shell command, it is used also to display all variables in the system, but it won't return any result in this case:

```
$ env | grep kevin
```

Environment variable

An environment variable is available globally in **the current shell**; it is seen by **all** commands and child sessions.

So to make the NAME variable an environment variable, we have to export it this way:

```
$ export NAME
```

Note: You can use 'export VARNAME=something' to create an environment variable in one shot.

After exporting the NAME variable, every command in **the current shell** can see it:

```
$ env | grep kevin
NAME=kevin


$ set | grep kevin
NAME=kevin


$ echo $NAME
kevin
```

We can use the unset command to remove a shell or an environment variable:

```
$ unset NAME
```

Type these commands to make sure the variable is removed:

```
$ set | grep kevin


$ env | grep kevin


$ echo $NAME
```

Process locality

The values of environment variables are local, which means they are specific to the running process in or for which they were set.

This means that if we open two terminal windows (which means we have two separate bash processes running), and change a value of an environment variable in one of the windows, that change will not be seen by the shell in the other window or any other program currently on the desktop.

Script files

A real world requirement is that system and user environment variables are set automatically immediately after users log in, that's when script files come in play.

At its most basic level, a script is a command or commands stored in a file. When the shell reads the file, it executes the commands as if you were entering them through the keyboard.

Here are some common script files in the order they execute, remember that settings in file that execute later in the process take precedence.

/etc/profile: this file executes immediately after a user logs in. It is a system wide initialization file that is used primarily to set **system** environment variables.

/etc/bashrc: this file executes after /etc/profile. It is also a system wide file that is often executed by individual users .bashrc file. It is most commonly used for aliases and functions.

~/.bash_profile or ~/bash_login or ~/.profile:

After /etc/profile executes, the system searches for these files in the user's home directory. These are optional files in which users can create settings specific to their systems.

~/.bash_profile executes first.

~/.bash_login only executes in the absence of ~/.bash_profile.

~/.profile only executes in the absence of the other two.

Real world scenario

In this section we'll manage to define an environment variable automatically every time a user logs in.

That environment variable will be accessed by a shell script we create.

Use these commands to create a simple shell script:

```
$ pwd
/home/Khaled Jamal


$ echo '#!/bin/sh' > my-script.sh


$ echo 'echo Hello ${MYNAME}' >> my-script.sh


$ chmod 755 my-script.sh
```

Execute the script like this:

```
$ ./my-script.sh
```

```
Hello
```

Note: to execute a script, grant yourself the execute permission using chmod (we'll talk about it later), then type the full path to the script, since the dot (.) refers to the current directory (/home/Khaled Jamal in our case) in which the script exists, we used simply ./my-script.sh.

The script looks for a non-existing environment variable called MYNAME, type this command to create it and re-execute:

```
$ MYNAME=Jamal
$ ./my-script.sh
Hello
```

It doesn't work because the script execution is a sub process and won't see a simple shell variable, we need to export it:

```
$ export MYNAME
$ ./my-script.sh
Hello Jamal
```

Now shut down the current shell (terminal), open a new one and run the script, it will display just 'Hello' because **the environment variable lives as long as the shell**.

 We need to make the export command in the ~/.bash_profile script which executes immediately after the user logs in, thus the environment variable will be created automatically.

Use the ls -a command to list bash scripts in your home directory, every user has **its own** profile scripts:

```
$ pwd
/home/ Khaled Jamal
$ ls -a
.  ..  .bash_history  .bash_profile  .bashrc .profile
```

Type the following command to add the environment variable to ~/.bash_profile:

```
$ pwd

/home/Khaled Jamal


$ echo export MYNAME=Jamal >> .bash_profile
```

Use the source command to reload ~/.bash_profile then execute the script: (Or shut down the terminal and open a new one then execute)

```
$ source .bash_profile

$ ./my-script.sh
Hello Jamal
```

Note: the dot can also be used to reload script files (the command would be . .bash_profile).

As long as you log in by that user account, the environment variable will be always available for you.

What happens if you log in by another user account and try to access MYNAME environment variable?

It won't show up, you must define it in ~/.bash_profile of that other user, or you can define it in /etc/profile and make it available to all users.

8 WILDCARDS

Commands can use wildcards to perform actions on more than one file at a time.

The asterisk *

The asterisk has the broadest meaning of any of the wildcards, as it can represent **zero or more characters**.

For example, **ls *.jpg** would tell the ls command to provide the names of all files in the current directory that have a .jpg extension.

Likewise, the following command would copy all files (in /etc) that have the string 'stab' in their names, to the /tmp directory:

```
$ cp -rfv /etc/*stab* /tmp
'/etc/fstab' -> '/tmp/fstab'
'/etc/fstab.d' -> '/tmp/fstab.d'


$ ls /tmp/*stab*
/tmp/fstab


/tmp/fstab.d:
```

Another example here where we list each entry (in /etc) that starts with the string 'bash':

```
$ ls -l /etc/bash*
-rw-r--r-- 1 … 856  1 Nov.   21:37 /etc/bash.bash_logout
-rw-r--r-- 1 … 1176 1 Nov.   21:37 /etc/bash.bashrc
```

What about listing all files that have a '.conf' extension:

```
$ ls -l /etc/*.conf
-rw-r--r-- 1 … 5139 1 Nov.   21:37 /etc/man_db.conf
-rw-r--r-- 1 …  393 1 Nov.   21:37 /etc/nsswitch.conf
```

Try to figure out how this command works:

Remember, the asterisk (*) represents zero or more characters, so /*/ means any directory under the root.

```
$ ls /*/*conf*
/bin/cyglsa-config  /bin/cygserver-config  /bin/getconf.exe
/etc/man_db.conf  /etc/nsswitch.conf
```

The question mark ?

The question mark (?) is used as a wildcard character to represent exactly one character.

In the following example we list each entry that has the string 'file' starting at the fourth position:

```
$ ls -l /etc/???file*
-rw-r--r--  1 … 5171  1 Nov.   21:37 /etc/profile

/etc/profile.d:
total 24
-rw-r--r-- 1 … 1107 20 Oct.   09:55 gawk.csh
-rw-r--r-- 1 …  757 20 Oct.   09:55 gawk.sh
…
```

Our command lists one file directly under /etc, its name is **profile**, and the content of the **/etc/profile.d** directory.

Square brackets []

The third type of wildcard is a pair of square brackets, which represent any of the characters enclosed in the brackets.

For example, the following would provide information about all objects that had an extension starting with b or c or i:

```
$ file /etc/*.[bci]*
/etc/bash.bash_logout: ASCII text
/etc/bash.bashrc:      ASCII text
/etc/man_db.conf:      ASCII text
/etc/nsswitch.conf:    ASCII text
/etc/rebase.db.i386:   data
```

When a hyphen is used between two characters in the square brackets wildcard, it indicates a range inclusive of those two characters.

The following would list all files starting with any letter from b through d:

```
$ cd /etc


$ ls [b-d]*
bash.bash_logout   bash.bashrc


defaults:
etc
```

Sometimes it can be useful to have a succession of square bracket wild-cards:

```
$ cd /etc


$ ls *.[a-ci-k][0-9]*
```

```
rebase.db.i386
```

The previous command displays all file names that had an extension starting with a **letter**:

From a to c, which means the first letter after the dot could be a or b or c

Or

From i to k, which means the first letter after the dot could be i or j or k

The letter will be followed by one digit from 0 to 9, and then followed by zero or more characters.

9 REGEX

A regular expression is a text string that describes a particular search pattern.

Different applications and programming languages implement regular expressions slightly differently. We'll explore a subset of the way that the grep command describes its patterns.

The caret ^

This symbol is for matching the beginning of line.

grep '^#' in the example below searches every line starting with '#' (in .bash_profile), and redirect its output to the head command to display just one line:

```
$ pwd
/home/Khaled Jamal


$ grep '^#' .bash_profile | head -1
# To the extent possible under law, the author(s) have dedi…
```

You can also look for lines starting with a string:

```
$ grep '^export' /etc/profile
export PROFILEREAD PATH ORIGINAL_PATH INFOPATH USER TMP TEMP …
```

The dollar $

This symbol is for matching the end of line.

In the following example, the find command brings all files and directories under /etc, the pipe sends the output to the grep command which displays just lines ending with the word 'profile':

```
$ find /etc | grep 'profile$'
/etc/defaults/etc/profile
/etc/defaults/etc/skel/.bash_profile
/etc/defaults/etc/skel/.profile
/etc/profile
/etc/skel/.bash_profile
/etc/skel/.profile
```

Note: don't worry we'll discuss the find command in another chapter.

The dot (.)

The dot is used in regular expressions to mean that any single character can exist at the specified location.

For example, if we want to match anything that has two characters between 'dedi' and 'ted', we can use the following pattern:

```
$ cat .bash_profile | grep 'dedi..ted'
# … possible under law, the author(s) have dedicated all
```

Square brackets []

We talked about it previously so let's take an example where we look for files ending with the letter a or b or c:

```
$ ls /etc | grep '[abc]$'
bash.bashrc
```

```
fstab
mtab
```

The dash within the square brackets operates as a range, so something like [a-cr-y] means either the letters:

a or **b** or **c**, or **r** or **s** or **t** or **y.**

The caret inside square brackets means that the character is **NOT** one of the included characters:

```
$ ls /etc | grep '[c-e][^abc]$'
alternatives
services
skel
```

Zero or more

There are two operators that indicate zero, one or more occurrences of the preceding characters:

The star (*): means that the preceding character can be repeated 0 or more times.

The plus (+): means that the preceding character can be repeated 1 or more times.

Suppose we want to find any line that begins with '#' and ends with a period, we can use the following expression:

```
$ cat .bash_profile | grep "^#.*\.$"
# ~/.bash_profile: executed by bash(1) for login shells.
# setup from updating it.
# a patch to the cygwin mailing list.
```

Let's decorticate the regex expression:

^# is for matching a # at the beginning of line.

.* the star after the dot means that any character could be repeated zero or more times.

\.$ is for matching a period at the end of line, the ending period is escaped so that it represents a literal period instead of the usual "any character" meaning.

Let's use the plus sign instead of the star:

```
$ cat .bash_profile | grep "^#.+\.$"
```

Nothing shows up, as if the plus sign didn't work.

Actually there are many types of regular expressions, we state:

The basic regular expression (BRE): ("^" , "$" , "*" , "." , "[]")

The extended regular expression (ERE): ("?" , "+", "{", "|", "(", ")")

As noted, the plus sign is one of the ERE operators, in order to use ERE with the grep command we should use the -E option:

```
$ cat .bash_profile | grep -E "^#.+\.$"
# ~/.bash_profile: executed by bash(1) for login shells.
# setup from updating it.
# a patch to the cygwin mailing list.
```

Another way to make it work is to escape the plus operator:

```
$ cat .bash_profile | grep "^#.\+\.$"
# ~/.bash_profile: executed by bash(1) for login shells.
# setup from updating it.
# a patch to the cygwin mailing list.
```

Rounded brackets ()

Rounded brackets are used to group several characters to behave as one.

Let's analyse the following command:

```
$ cat .bash_profile | grep -E 'HOME.*/(bin|etc)'
# if [ -d "${HOME}/bin" ] ; then
```

```
#    PATH="${HOME}/bin:${PATH}"
```

The command looks for lines that contain the string 'HOME', followed by zero or more characters (.*), followed by /, followed by bin or etc.

To indicate alternation, we use the pipe character "|". These are often used within parenthetical grouping to specify that one of two or more possibilities should be considered a match.

Suppose you want to modify the command in order to make the 'HOME' string as optional, to do that we'll use rounded brackets to group HOME's characters and apply an operator to them as a **unit**:

```
$ cat .bash_profile | grep -E '(HOME)?.*/(bin|etc)'

# always be found at /etc/defaults/etc/skel/.bash_profile

# Modifying /etc/skel/.bash_profile directly will prevent

# if [ -d "${HOME}/bin" ] ; then

#    PATH="${HOME}/bin:${PATH}"
```

The question mark we used above represents zero or one occurrence of the preceding unit (HOME).

10 FILTERS

In this chapter we'll learn the most common filters like grep, cut, tr, wc, sort, sed and awk.

grep

The grep command is used to filter lines of text, containing or not containing a certain specific string.

Let's prepare a file to experiment with this command:

```
$ pwd
/home/Khaled Jamal


$ echo This is the first line >> sample.txt
$ echo This is the second line >> sample.txt


$ cat sample.txt
This is the first line
This is the second line
```

The following command brings us only lines containing the 'first' string:

```
$ cat sample.txt | grep first
This is the first line
```

You can use grep directly by supplying the file name:

```
$ grep first sample.txt
This is the first line
```

grep with the i option ignores case distinctions in both the filtering <u>PAT-TERN</u> and the input files:

```
$ echo THIS IS THE THIRD LINE >> sample.txt

$ grep -i third sample.txt
THIS IS THE THIRD LINE
```

To select non-matching lines use the -v option:

```
$ grep -vi third sample.txt
This is the first line
This is the second line
```

To filter by many words, use quotes or double quotes:

```
$ grep -i 'the third' sample.txt
THIS IS THE THIRD LINE
```

And to search in all files in the current directory and its subdirectories, the -r (recursive) option is the one you need to use.

In the following example we're creating a tmp directory, and a notes.txt file into it:

```
$ cd
$ pwd
/home/Khaled Jamal

$ mkdir tmp
$ touch tmp/notes.txt
```

```
$ ls -R
.:
sample.txt   tmp

./tmp:
notes.txt
```

Then we add a few lines into notes.txt:

```
$ echo This is the first line >> tmp/notes.txt
$ echo This is the second line >> tmp/notes.txt

$ cat tmp/notes.txt
This is the first line
This is the second line
```

Finally we make use of the -r option to search recursively in the tmp directory:

```
$ grep -r 'the first' tmp
tmp/notes.txt:This is the first line
```

We can also use grep without the [FILE] argument to look recursively in the current directory:

```
$ cd
$ pwd
/home/Khaled Jamal

$ grep -r 'the first'
sample.txt:This is the first line
tmp/notes.txt:This is the first line
```

One important option to talk about is the -l option that print only file names containing matches.

Suppose we want to get only file names containing lines that start with the string 'export', let's look for that in all files under /etc:

```
$ grep -l '^export' /etc/*

grep: /etc/alternatives: Is a directory

/etc/bash.bashrc

grep: /etc/defaults: Is a directory

grep: /etc/fstab.d: Is a directory

grep: /etc/pkcs11: Is a directory

...
```

We got many error messages indicating **directories** that are not valid for this search, the -s option allows to suppress these error messages :

```
$ grep -sl '^export' /etc/*

/etc/bash.bashrc

/etc/profile
```

You can use the -r option to make a recursive search as well:

```
$ grep -srl '^export' /etc/*

/etc/bash.bashrc

/etc/defaults/etc/bash.bashrc

/etc/defaults/etc/profile

...
```

Obviously, if you remove the -l option you'll get a full result (file names and lines):

```
$ grep -sr '^export' /etc/*

/etc/bash.bashrc:export EXECIGNORE="*.dll"

/etc/defaults/etc/bash.bashrc:export EXECIGNORE="*.dll"

/etc/defaults/etc/profile:export PROFILEREAD PATH ORIGINAL...

...
```

cut

The cut command is used to extract portion of text from a file.

Go back to your home directory by typing cd:

```
$ cd
$ pwd
/home/Khaled Jamal
```

Use the following command to remove everything from the current directory:

```
$ rm -R *
$ ls -l
total 0
```

Create a file and fill it with a delimited text:

```
$ touch notes.txt
$ echo kevin:root:xw123 >> notes.txt
$ echo bruce:user:pass@q >> notes.txt

$ cat notes.txt
kevin:root:xw123
bruce:user:pass@q
```

Now let's use the cut command to extract logins and passwords:

```
$ cut -d: -f2,3 notes.txt
root:xw123
user:pass@q
```

The -d option is used to change the default delimiter.

The -f option specifies the second and third fields.

You can combine grep and cut commands to extract specific information:

```
$ grep kevin notes.txt | cut -d: -f2,3
root:xw123
```

When using a space as a delimiter for **cut**, you have to quote the space:

```
$ touch space-delimited.txt
$ echo This is the first line >> space-delimited.txt
$ echo This is the second line >> space-delimited.txt


$ cut -d' ' -f3-5 space-delimited.txt | tail -1
the second line
```

tr

The tr command is for translating, or deleting, or squeezing repeated characters.

The following example shows notes.txt content in upper case format and change the colon delimiter:

```
$ pwd
/home/Khaled Jamal


$ cat notes.txt | tr 'a-z' 'A-Z' | tr ':' ';'
KEVIN;ROOT;XW123
BRUCE;USER;PASS@Q
```

Let's empty the current directory and create a new file:

```
$ rm -R *
$ touch notes.txt


$ echo '-----This is the first line-----' >> notes.txt
$ cat notes.txt
-----This is the first line-----
```

You can use the -d (--delete) option to show a clean content by deleting this character '-':

```
$ cat notes.txt | tr -d -
This is the first line
```

Finally you can use the -s (--squeeze-repeats) option to replace multiple repeated spaces or characters by a single one:

```
$ echo 'This   is    the    second      line' >> notes.txt
$ cat notes.txt
-----This is the first line-----
This    is     the    second       line

$ cat notes.txt | tr -d - | tr -s ' '
This is the first line
This is the second line
```

wc

The wc (word count) command is used to find out number of new line count, word count, byte and characters count in a file.

The following command counts lines:

```
$ wc -l notes.txt
2 notes.txt
```

This one counts characters:

```
$ wc -c notes.txt
98 notes.txt
```

And this command counts words:

```
$ wc -w notes.txt
10 notes.txt
```

sort

The sort command is a utility for sorting lines of text files. It supports sorting alphabetically, in reverse order, by number, by month and can also remove duplicates.

The sort command sorts lines alphabetically by default:

```
$ pwd
/home/Khaled Jamal

$ rm -R *
$ touch notes.txt

$ echo 'Java
> Cobol
> C++
> Php
> Linux' > notes.txt

$ sort notes.txt
C++
Cobol
Java
Linux
Php
```

The sort command didn't change the file; it displays just its content in a sorted way. Type a cat notes.txt to make sure of that:

```
$ cat notes.txt
Java
Cobol
```

```
C++
Php
Linux
```

Use the -r option to sort in reverse order:

```
$ sort -r notes.txt
Php
Linux
Java
Cobol
C++
```

To sort and remove duplicates, pass the -u option (unique). This will write a sorted list to standard output and remove duplicates.

Let's append a duplicate entry to the file:

```
$ echo C++ >> notes.txt

$ cat notes.txt
Java
Cobol
C++
Php
Linux
C++

$ sort -u notes.txt
C++
Cobol
Java
Linux
```

Php

To sort by a delimiter pass the -t option, along with the delimiter value. This can be combined with the -k option to sort on fields within a CSV.

Here is an example:

```
$ touch notes.csv


$ echo "5;Java;Programming
> 3;SAP;ERP
> 1;Linux;System
> 4;Cisco;Networking" >> notes.csv


$ sort -t ";" -k 2 notes.csv
4;Ciso;Networking
5;Java;Programming
1;Linux;System
3;SAP;ERP


$ sort -t ';' -k 1 notes.csv
1;Linux;System
3;SAP;ERP
4;Cisco;Networking
5;Java,Programming
```

sed

sed is a stream editor that is used to perform basic text processing on a file or an input from a pipeline.

One of the most important uses of sed is substitution.

The substitute command changes all occurrences of a regular expression to a new value.

Type the following command to prepare the substitution.txt file:

```
$ cat /etc/profile | head -3 > substitution.txt


$ cat substitution.txt
# To the extent possible under law, the author(s) have …
# copyright and related and neighboring rights to this …
# public domain worldwide. This software is distributed …
```

The syntax of the substitution pattern is s/regex/replacement/.

So to substitute all # symbols at the beginning of line with a space use: (the replacement here is nothing)

```
$ sed 's/^#//' substitution.txt
 To the extent possible under law, the author(s) have …
 copyright and related and neighboring rights to this …
 public domain worldwide. This software is distributed …
```

You can make many substitutions by using the -e option, in the following example; we retain the last pattern and add a new one that replaces all occurrences of 'this' by 'THIS':

```
$ sed -e 's/^#//' -e 's/[tT]his/THIS/' substitution.txt
 To the extent possible under law, the author(s) have …
 copyright and related and neighboring rights to THIS …
 public domain worldwide. THIS software is distributed …
```

Note: [tT] is used to ignore the case.

The substitution is done by default on the first occurrence of the pattern **per line**, unless we add the g option.

The following command is supposed to replace all occurrences of 'the' by 'THE':

```
$ sed -e 's/^#//' -e 's/the/THE/' substitution.txt
 To THE extent possible under law, the author(s) have …
```

```
copyright and related and neighboring … software to THE

public domain worldwide. This software is distributed …
```

But there's a missing replacement on the first line (the author(s)), let's add the g option and retry:

```
$ sed -e 's/^#//' -e 's/the/THE/g' substitution.txt

To THE extent possible under law, THE author(s) have …

copyright and related and neighboring rights … software to THE

public domain worldwide. This software is distributed …
```

One important thing to talk about is the use of extended regular expression (ERE), checkout the regex chapter if you forgot it.

sed requires the -r or -E options to process ERE operators ("?" , "+" , "{" , "|" , "(" , ")").

The following example won't work without the -r or -E options, it replaces all occurrences of 'This' or 'this' by 'THIS':

```
$ sed -re 's/(This|this)/THIS/g' substitution.txt

# To the extent possible under law, the author(s) have …

# copyright and related and neighboring … THIS software to the

# public domain worldwide. THIS software is distributed …
```

You can do it also by escaping the ERE operators like this:

```
$ sed -e 's/\(This\|this\)/THIS/g' substitution.txt

# To the extent possible under law, the author(s) have …

# copyright and related and neighboring rights to THIS …

# public domain worldwide. THIS software is distributed …
```

Note that in all of the above examples we didn't change the substitution.txt file, let's check it:

```
$ cat substitution.txt

# To the extent possible under law, the author(s) have …

# copyright and related and neighboring … software to the
```

```
# public domain worldwide. This software is distributed …
```

The help informs us that the -i option allows editing files in place and can make backup if SUFFIX is supplied:

```
$ sed --help

Usage: sed [OPTION]... {script-only-if-no-other-script} [input-file]...

…

-i[SUFFIX], --in-place[=SUFFIX]

                edit files in place (makes backup if SUFFIX sup-plied)
```

The following example makes use of the -i option and supply a '_backup' suffix:

```
$ sed -i_backup -e 's/^#//' substitution.txt

$ ls

substitution.txt  substitution.txt_backup


$ cat substitution.txt

 To the extent possible under law, the author(s) have dedicated all

 copyright and related and neighboring rights to this software to the

 public domain worldwide. This software is distributed without any warranty.


$ cat substitution.txt_backup

# To the extent possible under law, the author(s) have dedicated all

# copyright and related and neighboring rights to this software to the

# public domain worldwide. This software is distributed without any warranty.
```

awk

awk is an advanced text processing utility, we'll discuss few notions that allow you to get deeper if you need to.

Use the echo command to prepare a csv file:

```
$ echo 'Kevin;Java;Junior

Bruce;C++;Senior

Jason;PHP;Senior' > test.csv
```

The following command extracts the **first** and **third** columns of the csv file, note that the default separator for awk is the white space, to change it, we use the -F option followed by a new separator enclosed in quotation marks:

```
$ awk -F';' '{print $1, $3}' test.csv

Kevin Junior

Bruce Senior

Jason Senior
```

You can also use the NF variable to get the last column, it's a built in variable that represents total number of fields in a record:

```
$ awk -F';' '{print $1,$NF}' test.csv

Kevin Junior

Bruce Senior

Jason Senior
```

Now that you have an idea of awk, check the syntax:

```
awk '/search pattern1/ {Actions}
     /search pattern2/ {Actions}' file
```

The search pattern is a regular expression. We didn't use it in the previous examples because it's optional.

The actions means the code to be executed upon the results (e.g. the print command in previous examples).

Several patterns and actions are possible.

In the examples below we're using search patterns to bring records according to multiple criteria.

This command looks for lines starting with the K letter:

```
$ awk -F';' '/^K/ {print $1 "\t" $2 "\t" $NF}' test.csv
Kevin    Java    Junior
```

This one looks for lines containing the java or Java strings:

```
$ awk -F';' '/[jJ]ava/ {print $1 "\t" $2 "\t" $NF}' test.csv
Kevin    Java    Junior
```

The last command looks for lines containing the java or Java or C++ strings:

```
$ awk -F';' '/([jJ]ava|C++)/ {print $1 "\t" $2 "\t" $NF}'
test.csv
Kevin    Java    Junior
Bruce    C++     Senior
```

The actions print all of the csv columns separated by a tab space (\t).

11 USEFUL TOOLS I

This chapter introduces tools to find and compress files, together with other common tools to execute commands as a background job.

find

This is a very useful command to search for files **recursively**.

If you simply type 'find' without any argument, all files in the current directory and its subdirectories will be listed:

```
$ pwd
/home/Khaled Jamal


$ find

.

./.bashrc

./.bash_history

./.bash_profile

./.inputrc

./.lesshst

./.minttyrc
```

```
./.profile
```

The following command looks for all files in the /etc directory as well as its subdirectories:

```
$ find /etc
/etc
/etc/alternatives
/etc/alternatives/README
/etc/bash.bashrc
/etc/bash.bash_logout
/etc/defaults
…
…
```

In the same locations, this command looks for all 'README' files:

```
$ find /etc -name README
/etc/alternatives/README
/etc/pki/ca-trust/extracted/java/README
/etc/pki/ca-trust/extracted/openssl/README
/etc/pki/ca-trust/extracted/pem/README
/etc/pki/ca-trust/extracted/README
/etc/pki/ca-trust/source/README
```

We can also use wildcards in the path as well as the pattern:

```
$ find /etc/s* -name "*.bash*"
/etc/skel/.bashrc
/etc/skel/.bash_profile
```

The command above searches **recursively** under /etc, in any directory whose name starts with the s letter.

It is often useful to ignore the case when searching for file names. To do that, use the "iname" option instead of the "name" option:

```
$ find /etc/s* -name "*.BASH*"


$ find /etc/s* -iname "*.BASH*"
/etc/skel/.bashrc
/etc/skel/.bash_profile
```

Sometimes we want to find only files or only directories with a given name.

For example, below we use the -type f option to look only for files:

```
$ find /etc -type f -iname "profile*"
/etc/defaults/etc/profile
/etc/profile
```

And we use -type d to look only for directories:

```
$ find /etc -type d -iname "profile*"
/etc/defaults/etc/profile.d
/etc/profile.d
```

we can search in many separate directories as well:

```
$ find /etc /home -type f -iname "*profile*"
/etc/defaults/etc/profile
/etc/defaults/etc/skel/.bash_profile
/etc/defaults/etc/skel/.profile
/etc/postinstall/base-files-profile.sh.done
/etc/profile
/etc/skel/.bash_profile
/etc/skel/.profile
/home/Khaled Jamal/.bash_profile
/home/Khaled Jamal/.profile
```

The find command not only looks for files based on a certain criteria, it can also act upon those files using any Linux command.

Say we want to list the result of the find command as ls would have done:

```
$ find /etc -type f -iname "profile*" -exec ls -l {} \;
-rwxr-xr-x 1 … Sep. 26  2015 /etc/defaults/etc/profile
-rw-r--r-- 1 … Nov.  1  21:37 /etc/profile
```

-exec: executes a command upon the found files (**{} \; is mandatory**).

Let's do another example that looks for certain folders and removes them using the -exec option:

```
$ pwd
/home/Khaled Jamal

$ mkdir folder1 folder2

$ find . -type d -iname "folder[1-2]" -exec rm -r {} \;

$ ls -l
total 0
```

Note: The dot after the find command, refers to the current directory.

gzip

The gzip command is a common way of compressing and uncompressing files.

Let's prepare a file to experiment with the gzip command:

```
$ pwd
/home/Khaled Jamal

$ ls -lhR /usr >> file-list.txt

$ ls -lh
```

```
total 652K

-rw-r--r-- 1 … 651K 14 Nov.   16:58 file-list.txt
```

Use the gzip command to compress the file (take note of the size):

```
$ gzip file-list.txt


$ ls -lh

total 84K

-rw-r--r-- 1 … 82K 14 Nov.   16:58 file-list.txt.gz
```

Use the -d option to decompress it:

```
$ gzip -d file-list.txt.gz


$ ls -lh

total 652K

-rw-r--r-- 1 … 651K 14 Nov.   16:58 file-list.txt
```

To keep the uncompressed file, use the -k option:

```
$ gzip -k file-list.txt


$ ls -lh

total 736K

-rw-r--r-- 1 … 651K 14 Nov.   16:58 file-list.txt
-rw-r--r-- 1 …  82K 14 Nov.   16:58 file-list.txt.gz
```

Let's delete the uncompressed file:

```
$ rm file-list.txt


$ ls -lh

total 84K

-rw-r--r-- 1 … 82K 14 Nov.   16:58 file-list.txt.gz
```

Then use the -k option to decompress the file while keeping the compressed one:

```
$ gzip -dk file-list.txt.gz


$ ls -lh
total 736K
-rw-r--r-- 1 … 651K 14 Nov.  16:58 file-list.txt
-rw-r--r-- 1 …  82K 14 Nov.  16:58 file-list.txt.gz
```

tar

The tar command is used to archive or distribute files. Tar archives can contain **multiple files and directories**, file permissions can be preserved and it supports multiple compression formats.

In the following example we're using the tar command to create a compressed archive of the /etc and /home directories:

```
$ pwd
/home/Khaled Jamal


$ tar pczf backup.tar.gz /etc /home


$ ls
backup.tar.gz
```

[p] This option stand for "preserve", it instructs tar to store details on file owner and file permissions in the archive.

[c] Stands for create. This option is mandatory when a file is created.

[z] The z option enables gzip compression.

[f] The f option tells tar that the next parameter is the file name of the archive.

The command to extract the backup is:

```
$ tar xzf backup.tar.gz

$ ls
backup.tar.gz   etc   home
```

[x] The x stand for extract, it is mandatory when a tar file shall be extracted.

[z] The z option tells tar that the archive to unpack is in a gzip format.

[f] The f option tells tar that the next parameter is the file name of the archive.

You can archive your files without using compression like we do in this example:

```
$ pwd
/home/Khaled Jamal

$ tar cvf archive.tar .bash*
.bash_history
.bash_profile
.bashrc
```

[v] This option stands for verbose; it tells tar to show all file names that get added into the archive.

If you want to extract an archive to a directory different from the current, use the -C option.

Let's create a directory and extract the archive into it:

```
$ pwd
/home/Khaled Jamal

$ mkdir extract
```

```
$ tar xvf archive.tar -C extract
.bash_history
.bash_profile
.bashrc


$ ls -a extract/
.  ..  .bash_history  .bash_profile  .bashrc
```

The ampersand (&)

The ampersand allows executing commands and shell scripts as a background job.

To demonstrate this, we'll create a shell script that prints welcome sentences every second in a log file.

Here are the commands to create and execute shell-script.sh:

```
$ pwd
/home/Khaled Jamal


$ echo '#!/bin/bash
> for i in {1..20}
> do
> echo "Welcome $i times" >> logs.txt
> sleep 1
> done' >> shell-script.sh


$ chmod 755 shell-script.sh


$ ./shell-script.sh
```

After executing the script, you have to wait 20 seconds until it finishes printing.

Now let's execute the shell script as a background job and still be able to look at the log file as it gets filled:

```
$ ./shell-script.sh &

[1] 4884


$ tail -f logs.txt

Welcome 17 times

Welcome 18 times

Welcome 19 times

Welcome 20 times

Welcome 1 times

Welcome 2 times

Welcome 3 times

…
```

We've used the tail command with the -f option to output appended data as the log file grows.

To quit the printing, press Ctr+c.

By the way, after you execute a command (or shell script) in the background using the ampersand (&), if you logout from the session, the command will get killed.

To avoid that, you should use the nohup command as shown below:

```
$ nohup ./shell-script.sh &
```

12 LINKS

Links are often used to store multiple copies of the same file in different places but still reference to one file.

Symbolic links

Symbolic links are like shortcuts or references to the actual file or directory, they are used all the time to link libraries and make sure files are in consistent places without moving or copying the original.

Any modification to the linked file will be changed on the original file. If you delete the link, the original file is unchanged, it will still exist, and if you delete the original file but not the link, the link will remain but will point to a file that does not exist.

We'll make an example to understand this concept.

Go into the /tmp directory and create a folder named practice, inside that folder, make a copy of /etc/profile:

```
$ cd /tmp

$ mkdir practice


$ cd practice/
```

```
$ cp /etc/profile profile


$ ls -ila profile
2251799814816612 -rw-r--r-- 1 … 8 Nov.  15:53 profile
```

The last command shows the copied file, take note of the **inode** at the first column. The inode is the physical reference on the hard drive where the file resides.

Now let's create a symbolic link called slinkprofile, it points to the profile file:

```
$ pwd
/tmp/practice


$ ln -s profile slinkprofile


$ ls -ila slinkprofile
20547673300372152 lrwxrwxrwx 1 … slinkprofile -> profile
```

Note how the **inode** for the link is different.

In the following example, we're editing the link to see if the changes will be made on the real file:

```
$ pwd
/tmp/practice


$ echo '#something' >> slinkprofile


$ tail -2 slinkprofile
export PROFILEREAD PATH ORIGINAL_PATH INFOPATH USER TMP …
#something
```

```
$ tail -2 profile
export PROFILEREAD PATH ORIGINAL_PATH INFOPATH USER TMP …
#something
```

Let's move /tmp/practice/profile and see if it causes any problems:

```
$ pwd
/tmp/practice

$ mv profile ../

$ cat slinkprofile
cat: slinkprofile: No such file or directory
```

After moving the original file, the symbolic link becomes broken as it is linked to a file name and not to the inode/physical location.

Keep in mind that symbolic links can reference a file or a folder on a different hard disk/volume; and that they reference abstract file-names/directories and NOT physical locations. They are given their own inode.

Hard links

This type differentiates from symbolic links by the following points:

They only link to a file not a directory.

They cannot reference a file on a different disk/volume.

They reference a file even if it is moved.

They reference **the inode/physical** locations on the disk.

Go to /tmp/practice, move back the profile file to its initial location (/tmp/practice) and create a hard link called hlinkprofile:

```
$ pwd
/tmp/practice
```

```
#move the file on the parent directory to the current one
$ mv ../profile .


$ ln profile hlinkprofile


$ ls -ila hlinkprofile profile
2251799814816612 -rw-r--r-- 2 … 8 Nov.  15:53 hlinkprofile
2251799814816612 -rw-r--r-- 2 … 8 Nov.  15:53 profile
```

Notice how the inode numbers are exactly the same for the hard link and the actual file.

Editing and saving the hard link would have the same effect on the original file as the symbolic link.

So let's move the original file:

```
$ pwd
/tmp/practice


$ mv profile ../


$ tail -2 hlinkprofile
export PROFILEREAD PATH ORIGINAL_PATH INFOPATH USER TMP …
#something
```

Looks like the hard link still work even though we moved the original file. This is because the hard link was linked to the inode, the physical reference on the hard drive where the file resides.

This leads to an interesting question. What happens if I delete a hard link?

Even though the hard link references the physical location of the file on the hard drive through an inode, removing a hard link will not delete the original file.

Type the following commands and see what happens:

```
$ pwd
/tmp/practice


$ rm hlinkprofile


$ ls ../
practice  profile
```

Use case

Let's create two long directory structures:

```
$ cd
$ pwd
/home/Khaled Jamal


$ mkdir -p project/linux/prod/l1/batch


$ mkdir -p project/linux/prod/l2/batch
```

You can make access easy by creating two symbolic links:

```
$ ln -s project/linux/prod/l1/batch l1batch


$ ln -s project/linux/prod/l2/batch l2batch


$ ls -l
total 2
lrwxrwxrwx  1 … l1batch -> project/linux/prod/l1/batch
lrwxrwxrwx  1 … l2batch -> project/linux/prod/l2/batch
```

Now, from anywhere you can easily access batch files, for example below, we're going to '/usr/lib/openssl-1.0.2/engines', then easily we access 'project/linux/prod/l1/batch' through the symbolic link created in our home directory:

```
$ cd /usr/lib/openssl-1.0.2/engines


$ cd ~/l1batch


$ touch extraction.sh tranformation.sh


$ ls

extraction.sh tranformation.sh


$ ls ~/project/linux/prod/l1/batch/

extraction.sh tranformation.sh
```

13 PERMISSIONS

Permissions specify what a particular person may or may not do with respect to a file or directory.

The mode

Every file has an inode that stores information about the file, including when the file was last modified, file size, data block location, permissions, and ownership (remember, directories are also files in the Linux system).

The portion of the inode that stores permission information is called the mode.

The mode has three sections, User permissions (owner), Group permissions (group owner), and other permissions (everyone on the Linux system).

There are three types of permissions contained in the mode:

Read(**r**): Allows to open and read the file, to list directory contents if the execute permission is also present.

Write(**w**): Allows to open, read and edit the file, as for directories it allows to add, delete and rename files if the execute permission is also present.

Execute(**x**): Allows executing the file (if it's a program file) or the shell script, for directories it allows to enter the directory and work with its contents.

When you identify permissions, you can either use the letter abbreviation (r, w, x), or the octal number that corresponds to the permission, the following graphic shows a detailed depiction of how permissions are displayed and how they can be referenced.

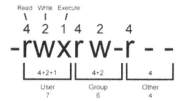

You should note the following facts about the mode:

A **d** preceding the permissions indicates that the object is a directory, a dash (-) identifies a file (the example above is for a file).

Permissions are grouped according to user, group, and other permissions.

If a permission has not been assigned, a dash (**-**) takes its place in order.

When using numbers to represent permissions, add the decimal numbers together within each permission group. Then string the numbers together. For example, the permissions in the graphic above can be represented by the number 764.

The root user has all permissions to files and directories regardless of what the mode indicates.

The chmod command

The chmod command (change mode, change permissions) allows modifying the permissions on a file.

It can be used in two ways: either by specifying the permissions in an octal way, using numbers; either by adding or removing permissions to one or more categories of users using the symbols r, w and x.

Let's create a shell script and try to execute it:

```
$ pwd
/home/Khaled Jamal


$ echo '#!/bin/sh' > my-script.sh


$ echo 'echo Hello' >> my-script.sh


$ ls -l
total 1
-rw-r--r-- 1 … 21 11 Nov.  22:42 my-script.sh
```

You, as the owner of this script have permissions to read and write (**rw-**), any group you belong to has a read permission (**r--**); everyone else in the system has the read permission (**r--**).

Try to execute the script like this:

```
$ ./my-script.sh
-bash: ./my-script.sh: Permission denied
```

A permission denied error occurs because initially you have no permission to execute the script, but since you are the owner, you can grant the execute permission to yourself and to everyone if you want.

That's what we're doing below, we're granting the execute permission (**x**) to the user (**u**), the group (**g**) he belongs to, and everyone (**o**):

```
$ chmod u+x,g+x,o+x my-script.sh


$ ls -l
total 1
-rwxr-xr-x 1 … 21 11 Nov.  22:42 my-script.sh
```

```
$ ./my-script.sh
Hello
```

You can remove the granted permission easily using this syntax:

```
$ chmod u-x,g-x,o-x  my-script.sh


$ ./my-script.sh
-bash: ./my-script.sh: Permission denied
```

In the following example we'll grant these permissions again, but this time we'll use the octal way, first of all type the ls -l command:

```
$ ls -l
total 1
-rw-r--r-- 1 … 21 11 Nov.   22:42 my-script.sh
```

Refer to the graphic to calculate the initial permission, it is 644, so to grant the execute permission we have to add 1 to each number:

```
$ chmod 755 my-script.sh


$ ls -l
total 1
-rwxr-xr-x 1 … 21 11 Nov.   22:42 my-script.sh
```

You can reset the initial permissions easily like this:

```
$ chmod 644 my-script.sh


$ ls -l
total 1
-rw-r--r-- 1 … 21 11 Nov.   22:42 my-script.sh
```

One important thing to talk about is the R option; it is used to change files and directories permissions **recursively**.

Suppose you want to grant all users the write permission for the content of your folder.

Firstly, create a folder and two files into it:

```
$ cd /tmp


$ mkdir jamal-folder


$ touch jamal-folder/notes.txt jamal-folder/contacts.txt
```

As you see below, other users have just the read and execute permissions on the folder we've created:

```
$ ls -ld jamal-folder/
drwxr-xr-x+ 1 … 0 13 Dec.  23:59 jamal-folder/


$ ls -l jamal-folder/
total 0
-rw-r--r-- 1 … 0 13 Dec.   23:59 contacts.txt
-rw-r--r-- 1 … 0 13 Dec.   23:59 notes.txt
```

Use the R option to grant them the write permission on the folder and all its content recursively:

```
$ chmod -R o+w jamal-folder/


$ ls -ld jamal-folder/
drwxr-xrwx+ 1 … 0 13 Dec.  23:59 jamal-folder/


$ ls -l jamal-folder/
total 0
-rw-r--rw- 1 … 0 13 Dec.  23:59 contacts.txt
-rw-r--rw- 1 … 0 13 Dec.  23:59 notes.txt
```

14 VI EDITOR

The vi editor is a tool to put content into files and edit that content as well. It operates in two basic modes, command mode and insert mode. When vi is started, it is in command mode.

The command mode allows you to move around the file, perform actions such as deleting, copying, search and replace, saving, however, you can only insert text by using the insert mode.

From command mode, you can enter into insert mode by typing the letter i or a. To return to command mode, use the **Escape** key (**sometimes you need to hit it more than once**).

Navigate

In the following example we're redirecting the list of all files in /bin, to file-list.txt:

```
$ pwd
/home/Khaled Jamal


$ ls -lh /bin > file-list.txt
```

Type 'vi file-list.txt' and press enter, as we said, when vi is started, it is in command mode.

Try to practice all the following commands by editing this file or another of your choice, it's very important.

Let's learn how to navigate through the file; obviously arrow keys move the cursor as they do in other editors.

Here are the most common navigation commands for moving around the current line:

0   Move to the beginning of the current line.

$ Move to the end of the current line.

w   Move to the beginning of the next word.

b   Move backwards to the beginning of the previous word.

Here are the most common navigation commands for moving around the current screen:

H   Move to the first line on the screen.

M   Move to the middle line of the screen.

L   Move to the last line of the screen.

And here are the most common navigation commands for moving around the overall file:

G   Move to the last line of the file.

1G Move to the first line of the file.

[Ctrl]f   Move forward one screen.

[Ctrl]b   Move backward one screen.

Delete and replace

Here are the most common commands for deleting characters:

x   delete the character below the cursor.

X   delete the character before the cursor.

r   replace the character below the cursor.

Notice that the r key will bring you in insert mode for **just one key press** to type your new character, and will return you immediately to command mode.

Undo and repeat

When in command mode, you can undo your mistakes with u. You can repeat your last command with the dot.

u   undo the last action.

.   repeat the last action.

Cut, copy and paste a line

With the cursor at your desired line press yy to copy this line. Press p wherever you like and the line will be pasted below the line you are on.

Likewise, with the cursor at your desired line press dd to cut this line. Press p wherever you like and the line will be pasted below the line you are on. d stands for "delete" and you can use dd to delete a line also.

Here are the commands:

dd   cut the current line

yy   copy the current line

p   paste after the current line

P   paste before the current line

The same way you can copy multiple lines just by typing a number before dd or yy, for example 3yy will copy three lines starting from the one with the cursor.

Join or add blank lines

Pressing J will append the next line to the current line, give it a try.

Pressing o or O will add a blank line and go into insert mode so you can add text. Use the escape key to return to command mode.

Leave vi

Pressing the colon (:) allow you to give instructions to vi:

:w   will write (save) the file.

:q! will quit vi discarding any changes.

:wq will save and quit.

To save your current file as another file use:

:w fileName

Search

While in command mode:

Type / (slash).

Enter the text to search for.

Press <Enter>.

The cursor moves to the first occurrence of that text.

To repeat the search in a forward direction, type: n

To repeat the search in a backward direction, type: N

Search and replace

To do this operation you have to switch to ex mode by pressing colon key (:)

From this vi mode You can do simple things, like quitting your vi session, like this:

:q! or :wq!

Or you can issue Linux commands from within your vi editor session, like this simple ls command:

:!ls

It's really handy sometimes to be able to stay in your vi editing session but still be able to run Linux commands.

You can also perform search and replace commands. So to replace all occurrences of the string old with new, as we said press colon key, then type the following command:

```
:1,$ s/old/new/g
```

1,$: will do the replace all from **the first** to the **last line**. You can write 1,5 to only process the first five lines.

s/old/new/g: will replace all occurrences of old with new.

Insert mode

Remember that when you first start vi like this:

vi [filename]

You are initially in command mode. Here are the commands to enter insert mode so you can type text into your file:

i   insert text before cursor, until <Esc> hit.

a   append text after cursor, until <Esc> hit.

A very important concept to know is that when you're in vi insert mode, you can easily move back to command mode by pressing the [Esc] key.

15 BASH SCRIPTING I

The shell is a command line interpreter that provides access to the internal functionalities of an operating system.

On most Linux systems, a program called bash acts as the shell. Besides bash, there are other shell programs that can be installed on a Linux system (e.g. sh, ksh, csh, tcsh, zsh).

We'll study bash because it's found by default on Linux, makes scripting simpler than sh and it's more common than ksh and zsh.

Scripting chapters assume prior programming knowledge.

Setting up the scripting environment

We continue to use Cygwin, Firstly type the commands below to set up a bash script:

```
$ pwd
/home/Khaled Jamal


$ touch bash-script.sh


$ chmod 755 bash-script.sh
```

In following sections, you can use vi or Notepadd++ to write bash programs.

Note: to use Notepadd++, look for your script on the default installation location of Cygwin, in my case it's C:\cygwin\home\Khaled Jamal. After editing the script, execute from Cygwin terminal. If it doesn't work, make use of 'Convert to UNIX format' on the Edit menu under EOL Conversion, then 'Encode in ANSI' on the Format menu, after that save and re-try.(anyway be careful of encoding errors)

We're going to use the truncate command to empty the bash script from time to time:

```
$ truncate -s 0 bash-script.sh
```

Variables

Let's code this example to talk about variables:

We want to mention that **formatting** is very important in bash scripting; note that there's no space or empty lines around the first line, nor on either sides of the equals (=) sign.

```
#!/bin/bash

subject=Greeting

recipient=Kevin

message="Hello $recipient, I hope you are well"

signature='Khaled Jamal'

echo $subject
echo
echo $message
```

```
echo

echo $signature
```

The first line indicates the path to the program that should be used to interpret the rest of lines in the script (bash in our case); it must be on the very first line with no spaces around or in between.

Then, three variables are set and printed using the basic equal sign (with no spaces around) and echo command.

To read a variable we place its name preceded by a $ sign. ${variable} is another syntax used as a disambiguation mechanism, so you can say ${dir}01072018 when you mean the content of the variable dir followed by 01072018, as opposed to $dir01072018 which means, the content of the variable dir01072018.

To make variables store more than one word, we need to use quotes (e.g. the signature variable).

Double quotes must be used to allow referencing variables within variable's value (e.g. we referenced $recipient in the value of the message variable).

Execute the script:

```
$ ./bash-script.sh

Greeting


Hello Kevin, I hope you are well


Khaled Jamal
```

In addition to normal variables set by users, bash has some built in variables that are pre-set by the system.

Let's empty the bash script and write this code:

```
#!/bin/bash

echo
```

```
echo The name of the current script is $0

echo

echo Here are the command line supplied arguments: $1 - $2

echo

echo The process ID of the current script is $$

echo

echo The username of the current user is $USER
```

Execute the script, this time we supply two arguments arg1, arg2:

```
$ ./bash-scripting.sh arg1 arg2


The name of the current script is ./bash-scripting.sh


Here are the command line supplied arguments: arg1 - arg2


The process ID of the current script is 12228


The username of the current user is Khaled Jamal
```

The example explains itself, notice that you can supply up to 9 arguments to the bash script (from $1 to $9).

One last thing to talk about before finishing this section is command substitution, this simply allows to assign a command's result to a variable, to do this we place the command within rounded brackets, preceded by a $ sign.

Here is an example:

```
#!/bin/bash


result=$(ls -l /etc | grep '^d' | wc -l)


echo There are $result directories under /etc
```

```
echo
echo There are $(ls -l /etc | grep '^d' | wc -1) directories un-
der /etc
```

$(command) can be used directly to evaluate a command and return its output (as we did in the last line).

Execute the script:

```
$ ./bash-scripting.sh
There are 11 directories under /etc


There are 11 directories under /etc
```

There's another form that uses back quotes (instead of $ and rounded brackets):

```
$ echo There are `ls -l /etc | grep '^d' | wc -1` directories
under /etc


There are 11 directories under /etc
```

Command substitution is useful if the command output is a single word or line.

Conditions

The basic syntax of an if statement is:

```
if [ test ]
then
    echo "Hello"
fi
```

Again, formatting is very important, note the spaces around the 'test' condition, and that 'then' should be written on a new line.

To write 'then' on the same line, you must add a semicolon after the brackets, actually it's another syntax you might encounter, here it is:

```
if [ test ]; then
    echo "Hello"
fi
```

Let's empty the bash script and make this example:

```
#!/bin/bash

directories=$1

if [ "$directories" = '/etc /dev' ]
then
    ls $directories
fi
```

The code is very simple, we assign a given argument ($1) to a variable and then compare this variable against '/etc /dev', if it's true, we run ls /etc /dev, else we do nothing.

Execute the script by supplying the '/etc /dev' argument:

```
$ ./bash-script.sh '/etc /dev'
/dev:
clipboard conout dsp full mqueue ptmx random sda sda2 shm …

/etc:
alternatives bash.bashrc DIR_COLORS fstab.d man_db.conf …
```

To do something when the condition is not met, you can use the 'else' keyword like this:

```
#!/bin/bash

directories=$1

```

```
if [ "$directories" = '/etc /dev' ]
then
    ls $directories
else
    ls /
fi
```

Let's supply an argument that triggers the else block:

```
$ ./bash-script.sh something
bin  cygdrive  Cygwin.bat  Cygwin.ico  Cygwin-Terminal.ico  desk-
top  dev  etc  home  lib  proc  sbin  tmp  usr  var
```

Here are the different types of test you can perform on strings:

$str1 = $str2: check if both strings are identical.

$str1 != $str1: check if both strings are different.

-z $str: check if the string is empty.

-n $str: check if the string is not empty.

For example, in the following program, we use the -z option to check if an argument exists:

```
#!/bin/bash


if [ -z $1 ]
then
    echo 'No given argument'
else
    echo $1
fi
```

Execute the script:

```
$ ./bash-scripting.sh
```

```
No given argument

$ ./bash-scripting.sh something

something
```

By default, bash handles all variables as strings, but nothing prevents from making number comparisons if these variables contain numbers.

Here are the different types of test we can perform with numeric variables:

$n1 -eq $n2: check if the numbers are equal. Not to be confused with the "=" which compares two strings.

$n1 -ne $n2: check if the numbers are different. Not to be confused with "!=" which compares two strings.

$n1 -lt $n2: checks if n1 is lower than n2.

$n1 -le $n2: checks if n1 is lower than or equal to (<=) n2.

$n1 -gt $n2: checks if n1 is greater (>) than n2.

$n1 -ge $n2: checks if n1 is greater than or equal to (> =) n2.

In the following example, we're comparing numbers as well as introducing the elif keyword which simply means else if:

```
#!/bin/bash

number=$1

if [ $number -eq 100 ]
then
    echo "$number = 100"
elif [ $number -gt 100 ]
then
```

```
    echo "$number > 100"
elif [ $number -lt 100 ]
then
    echo "$number < 100"
fi
```

Execute the script with different arguments:

```
$ ./bash-script.sh 100
100 = 100


$ ./bash-script.sh 20
20 < 100


$ ./bash-script.sh 200
200 > 100
```

The last type of tests is about files, we can check if they exist, if they're editable or executable and more.

Here are the different types of test we can do in this direction:

-e $filename: check if the file exists.

-d $filename: check if the file is a directory.

-f $filename: check if the file is a file.

-L $filename: check if the file is a symbolic link.

-w $filename: check if the file is editable (w).

-x $filename: check if the file is executable (x).

The following program performs few tests over a given argument that is supposed to be a file or a directory:

Note: $# is a built in variable that represents the number of parameters passed to the script.

```
#!/bin/bash


if [ $# -ge 1 ]
then
    if [ -e $1 ] && [ -d $1 ]
    then
        echo $1 is a directory
    elif [ -e $1 ] && [ -f $1 ]
    then
        echo $1 is a file
    else
        echo $1 doesn\'t exist
    fi
else
    echo No given argument
fi
```

Let's execute with different arguments:

```
$ ./bash-script.sh
No given argument

$ ./bash-script.sh /etc/fstab
/etc/fstab is a file

$ ./bash-script.sh /bin
/bin is a directory

$ ./bash-script.sh /system
/system doesn't exist
```

16 BASH SCRIPTING II

This chapter introduces two basic elements of all programming languages: loops and functions.

Loops

Loops allow repeating as many times as necessary a part of code.

The program below is an example of a while loop:

```
#!/bin/bash

index=1

while [ $index -lt 6 ]
do
    printf "$index "
    sleep 1
    let index++
done
```

Note: either you type the **do keyword** on a new line, else you should add a semicolon after the brackets (while [$index -lt 6]; do):

The code prints numbers from 1 to 5 every second:

```
$ ./bash-script.sh
1 2 3 4 5
```

The program below does the same thing by using a for loop:

```
#!/bin/bash

for index in {1..5}
do
    printf "$index "
    sleep 1
    let index++
done
```

Another example here that iterates over a command's result:

```
#!/bin/bash

index=1

for e in $( ls / | grep -iv ^c )
do
    echo Entry ${index}: $e
    let index++
done
```

The execution prints the names of directories not starting with the letter c:

```
$ ./bash-script.sh
Entry 1: bin
Entry 2: desktop
Entry 3: dev
```

```
Entry 4: etc

Entry 5: home

Entry 6: lib

Entry 7: proc

...
```

I want to mention that you can write all of this code in the terminal using semicolons like this:

```
$ index=1;for e in $(ls / | grep -iv ^c); do echo Entry
${index}: $e;let index++;done
Entry 1: bin

Entry 2: desktop

Entry 3: dev

Entry 4: etc

Entry 5: home

...
```

Functions

A function is a set of instructions, allowing to perform several tasks. They make your program more readable and structured. In addition, you can call your function as many times as you want in your script.

The following program defines two functions with different syntaxes that are all correct:

```
#!/bin/bash


#This is a way to define a function
executepwd (){
    echo The current working directory is $(pwd)
}
```

```
#This is another way to define a function
function executeps {
    echo Processes currently on the system:
    ps
}


echo
executepwd
echo
executeps
```

As you see **in the last lines**, calling a function is a matter of typing its name, let's execute and see the result:

```
$ ./bash-scripting.sh


The current working directory is /home/Khaled Jamal


Processes currently on the system:
      PID    PPID    PGID    WINPID   TTY          UID     STIME COMMAND
     4720    6732    4720       840   pty0     1539555  15:52:56 /usr/bin/bash
    11056    4720    4720      8004   pty0     1539555  15:52:56 /usr/bin/ps
     6732    1524    6732      9796   pty0     1539555   Jan  8 /usr/bin/bash
     1524       1    1524      1524   ?        1539555   Jan  8 /usr/bin/mintty
```

We can pass parameters to functions as we pass them to scripts, in the following example we define a function that counts directories in a direc-tory passed as an argument (**/etc**):

```
#!/bin/bash


countDirectories() {
    local count=$(ls -l $1 | grep '^d' | wc -l)
    echo There are $count directories under $1
```

```
}

echo
countDirectories /etc
```

The execution output is:

```
$ ./bash-scripting.sh


There are 11 directories under /etc
```

Let's modify the program in such a way to provide the argument at the script level, which is more flexible:

```
#!/bin/bash

countDirectories() {
    local count=$(ls -l $1 | grep '^d' | wc -l)
    echo There are $count directories under $1
}

echo
countDirectories $1
```

The execution output is:

```
$ ./bash-scripting.sh /dev


There are 2 directories under /dev


$ ./bash-scripting.sh /etc


There are 11 directories under /etc
```

One more important thing to talk about is local variable. Briefly, in a function, a variable declared as **local** is visible only within that function.

The program below clearly demonstrates the concept:

```
#!/bin/bash


printMessage() {
    local name=Kevin
    echo Hello $name
}


# This is a global variable
name=Bruce


# printMessage will print the closest local variable (name)
printMessage


# This will print Bruce and not Kevin because local
# variables are not visible outside functions in which
# they are declared
echo Hello $name
```

The execution output is:

```
$ ./bash-scripting.sh
Hello Kevin
Hello Bruce
```

Here document

A here document is used to redirect input into an interactive shell script or program.

The general form for a here document is:

```
command << delimiter

text or commands

delimiter
```

The shell interprets the (<<) operator as an instruction to read input until it finds a line containing the specified delimiter. All input lines up to the line containing the delimiter are then fed into the standard input of the command.

The delimiter tells the shell that the **here** document has completed. Without it, the shell continues to read the input forever. The delimiter must be a single word that does not contain spaces or tabs.

The following example gives an idea about it, the text lines between the eof delimiters are sent to the cut command which retrieves the first field:

```
$ cut -d';' -f1 << eof

bruce;java

kevin;linux

eof


bruce

kevin
```

Now that we've talked about text lines, what about feeding a list of commands to an interactive program or command.

Firstly we're going to create two files, demo1.txt and demo2.txt:

```
$ cd


$ pwd

/home/Khaled Jamal


$ echo Hello Kevin > demo1.txt

```

```
$ echo Hello Bruce > demo2.txt


$ cat demo1.txt demo2.txt

Hello Kevin

Hello Bruce
```

Suppose you need to iterate over all text files in the current user's home directory, and to edit each file by substituting the string Hello by Hi.

The following script can do it automatically, it iterates over the fgrep result and executes vi upon each file, we make use of the here document mechanism to feed commands to the vi current session:

```
#!/bin/bash


ORIGINAL=Hello

REPLACEMENT=Hi


for word in $(fgrep -l $ORIGINAL ~/*.txt)

do

  # Feeding two commands to every vi session

  vi $word <<EOF

          :%s/$ORIGINAL/$REPLACEMENT/g

          :wq

EOF

#The delimiter above must NOT be preceded by a space

done
```

Execute the script and check the files:

```
./bash-scripting.sh
$ cat demo1.txt demo2.txt

Hi Kevin

Hi Bruce
```

By the way it was just a demonstration to clarify the concept, in real world you would use a filter like this one:

```
$ sed -ie 's/Hi/Hello/g' $(fgrep -il 'Hi' ~/*.txt)


$ cat demo1.txt demo2.txt

Hello Kevin

Hello Bruce
```

17 SETTING UP A LINUX ENVIRONMENT

This chapter is a step by step demonstration of a Linux environment installation.

I installed this environment many times to be sure it will work for you but anyway if you encounter any problem, please make a google search and fix it.

Installing VirtualBox

Virtualization is about running multiple operating systems on a single machine, while giving the perfect illusion that they are on different physical computers.

There are many tools for managing virtual machines; VirtualBox is the one we're going to use.

You need to download the VirtualBox installer here:

http://www.oracle.com/technetwork/server-storage/virtualbox /downloads/index.html

Double click the executable, keep the default setting and install Virtual-Box.

When installation completes, double click the VirtualBox icon on your desktop. You should see something like this:

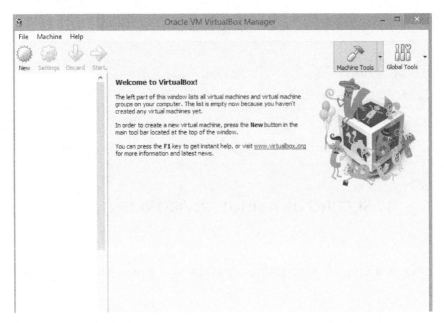

Creating a Virtual Machine

To create a virtual machine click New, inside that virtual machine we'll install the Ubuntu operating system, so name it Ubuntu, Choose a Linux type and the version (32bit or 64bit according to your machine).

Click next and select a great amount of RAM memory but don't exceed the green line.

Click next and choose to create a virtual hard disk now.

Click next and choose VDI (VirtualBox Disk Image).

Click next and choose dynamically allocated.

Click next and select the size of your virtual hard disk, 10 GB or 15 GB is enough.

Click Create.

Installing Ubuntu

You need to download The Ubuntu ISO file here:

https://www.ubuntu.com/download/desktop

When done, go back to VirtualBox and select the created VM then click Settings:

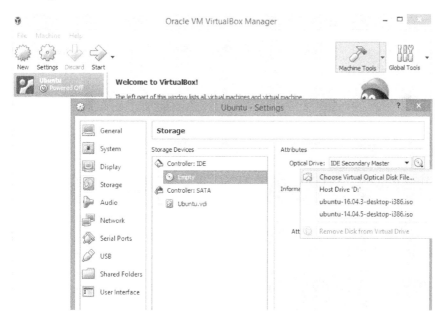

Select the Storage menu, select Empty, click on the CD icon on the right and click Choose Virtual Optical Disk File, select your downloaded ISO file.

Select the System menu and change the boot order to be like this, after that click OK:

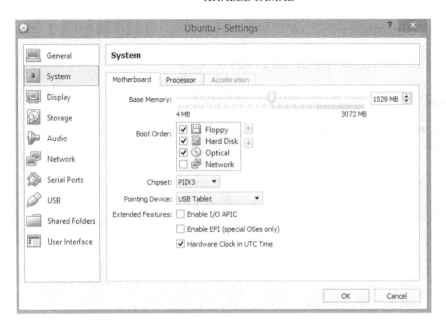

Your virtual machine is now ready, select it from the list and click Start! The installation of your operating system begins, you will be asked to choose whether to try Ubuntu or Install it, choose Install Ubuntu.

Keep the default and click continue till you come at this screen

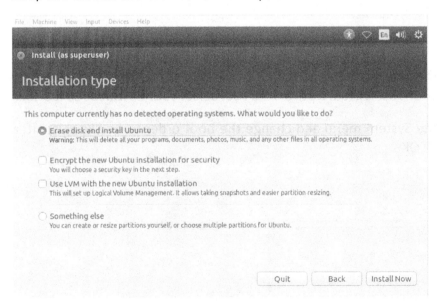

Don't worry, keep the Erase disk and install Ubuntu option, click Install

Now. A confirmation window might show up, just click Continue.

Choose your location and click Continue.

Choose your keyboard layout and click Continue.

Enter your name, a username and a password and click Continue (take note of the username and the password).

The final stage is to wait for the files to finish copying and the installation to complete.

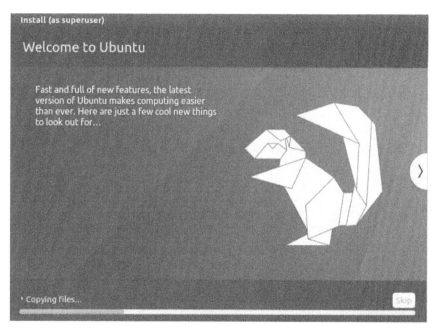

When the process is complete, you will be asked to reboot. This, of course, refers to the virtual machine and not your host Windows machine.

Click Restart Now.

Setting up networking

In this section we'll setup networking and share internet connection between the host and the guest.

The host: the operating system on which VirtualBox is installed.

The guest: Ubuntu in our case.

Go to Control panel, then to Network connections, do you notice a new connection named 'Virtual Box Host-Only Network'? It is added when you installed VirtualBox and will be used for networking issues.

Let's begin by sharing Internet connection, right click your internet connection, and then click on Sharing panel:

Check 'Allow other network users to connect through this computer's Internet connection'.

Choose 'Virtual Box Host-Only Network'.

Click OK.

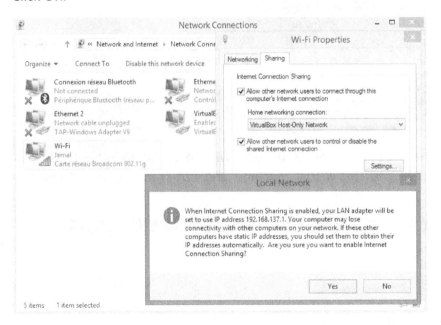

The message informs you that the VirtualBox connection will be set up to use IP address 192.168.137.1.

Click Yes.

Note: The number 137 might be something else in your system, whatever it is, keep note of it because we'll use it later.

We have to configure the virtual machine to use VirtualBox connection. Go back to VirtualBox, select the Ubuntu VM and click Settings.

Select the Network menu and choose the following configuration:

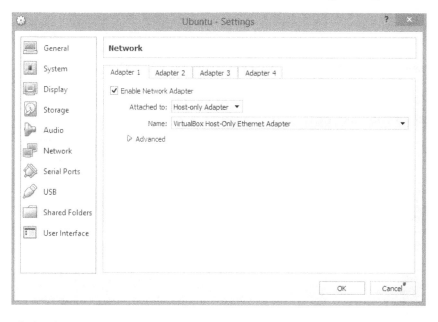

Click Ok.

Click start, when Ubuntu get started, right click the networking icon on the top right and click Edit Connections...

A small window appears, select 'Wired connection 1' and click Edit.

On the IPv4 Settings panel, choose a Manual Method, click Add and enter an IP configuration like this:

Substitute 137 with whatever you got when you shared the Internet connection.

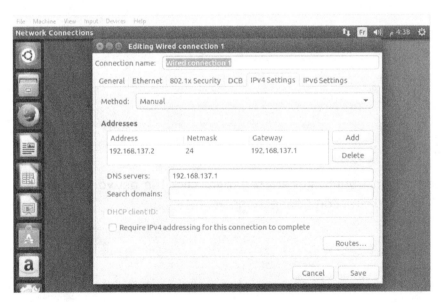

Click Save.

To test connectivity:

Click the start menu on Windows, in the Search or Run line, type cmd, press enter and type:

```
ping 192.168.137.2 -t
```

Switch back to Ubuntu, Click the button on the left top and type Terminal:

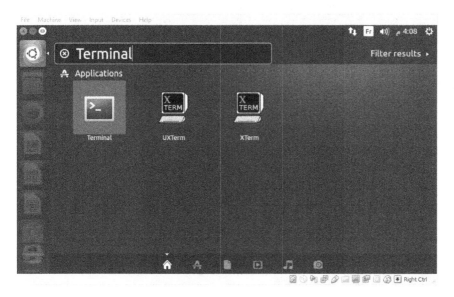

Run the terminal and type this command:

```
ping 192.168.137.1
```

If you don't get a reply from either side, right click the networking icon on the top right and uncheck 'Enable Networking'.

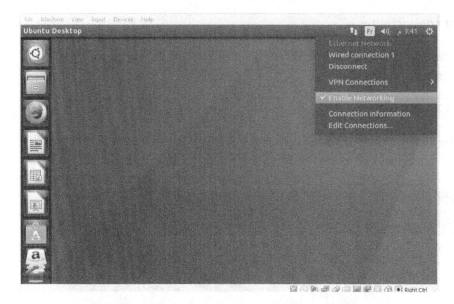

Right click on that icon again and check 'Enable Networking'.

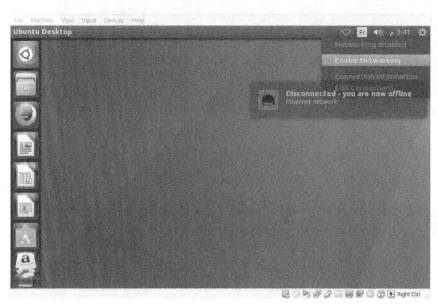

Keep doing that till you get a reply in the Windows or Ubuntu console.

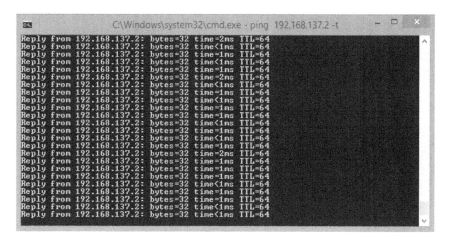

Note: if it doesn't work, disable the firewall else, try to analyze the problem, search on google and make it work.

Installing Putty

Putty is an SSH and telnet client, the point is to install it on your host operating system and connect remotely to Ubuntu VM.

You can download it here http://www.putty.org/, the installation is very simple, just do it.

To make an SSH client connection to Ubuntu, you need to install openssh-server (on Ubuntu), run the terminal and type the following command:

```
$ sudo apt-get update

...

Fetched 30.6 MB in 2min 7s (239 kb/s)

Reading package lists... Done
```

Note: apt-get requires a super user's privileges; a shortcut to do it without switching to root, is the sudo command that allows running a program as a super user.

Wait for the command to finish then type:

```
$ sudo apt-get install openssh-server
```

When it's finished, go to the host desktop, double click Putty icon, enter the guest IP address and click Open, after that click Yes.

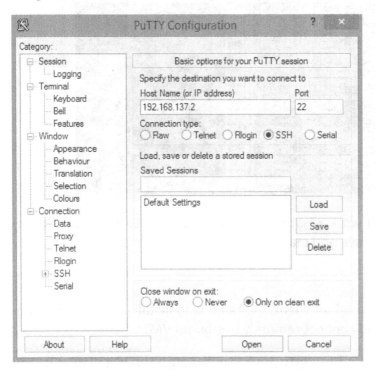

Enter the username and password you've set during Ubuntu installation, and that's it, now you're connected to Ubuntu remotely from your host operating system:

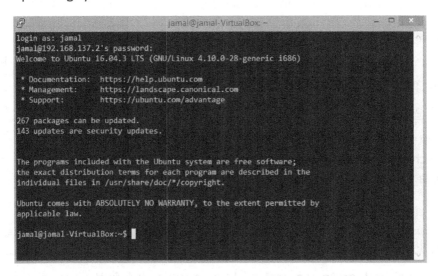

Installing WinSCP

WinSCP is an open source graphical SFTP client for Windows. The purpose of this program is to allow secure copy of files between a local computer and a remote computer.

Download the WinSCP installer here https://winscp.net, keep default settings and install it.

Double click the WinSCP icon on your desktop; enter the guest IP address, the username and the password, then click Login, click Yes if you get another window.

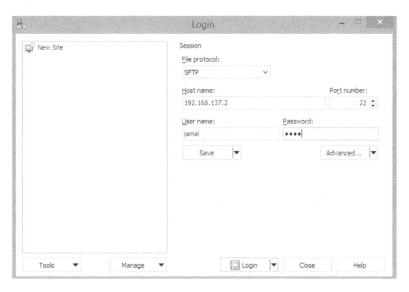

The program allows copying files between windows and Linux just by using drag and drop from right to left and inversely.

There is also a very interesting 'Find files' functionality to work with. It does the same thing as the find command.

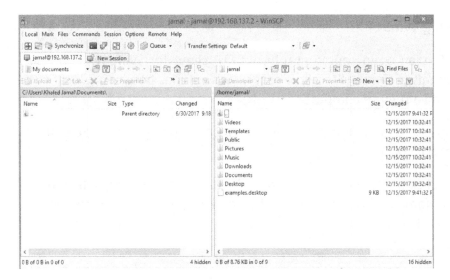

This is a very popular tool, try to get familiar with.

Note: we'll use this environment in the next chapters.

18 USEFUL TOOLS II

This chapter introduces tools to download and install software, as well as tools to monitor processes and disk usages.

The last section is dedicated to ownership.

apt-get

Linux don't have installation programs (.exe) like windows; it has what we call packages.

A package is a kind of zipped folder that contains all the program files. It is in the form of a .deb file. It contains all the necessary instructions to install the program.

It is very rare for a program to work alone on Linux. Very often, it uses other programs or other "bits of programs" called libraries. We say programs have dependencies.

Fortunately, the Debian package system is smart. Each package indicates which other packages it depends on.

This allows the system to recover missing dependencies automatically if needed.

All packages are grouped together in one place called a repository. This is a server that offers all the packages that exist (or almost), which greatly simplifies your search.

By default, when you install Ubuntu, it uses the official repositories of the distribution.

To get the list of repositories you use, type the following command:

```
jamal@jamal-VirtualBox:~$ grep "^[^#]" /etc/apt/sources.list
deb http://ma.archive.ubuntu.com/ubuntu/ xenial main restricted
deb http://ma.archive.ubuntu.com/ubuntu/ xenial-updates main …
…
```

Let's start by updating the package cache. This corresponds to downloading the new list of packages offered by the repositories.

To update your cache, type:

```
jamal@jamal-VirtualBox:~$ sudo apt-get update
[sudo] password for jamal:
Hit:1 http://ma.archive.ubuntu.com/ubuntu xenial InRelease
Get:2 http://ma.archive.ubuntu.com/ubuntu xenial-updates …
…
```

Note that you don't need to run this command every time you want to install a package but only from time to time to make sure you have the most up-to-date list.

And unless you already know the exact name of the package you want, you will have to do a little search.

The following command performs a package search in your cache. This avoids having to go on the Internet to do the research, which would have been slow. Below we're looking for a graphical ftp client:

```
jamal@jamal-VirtualBox:~$ apt-cache search graphical ftp client
filezilla - Full-featured graphical FTP/FTPS/SFTP client
gftp-gtk - X/GTK+ FTP client
```

```
...
```

For example to install the filezilla ftp client, use the apt-get install command like this:

```
jamal@jamal-VirtualBox:~$ sudo apt-get install filezilla

[sudo] password for jamal:

Reading package lists... Done

Building dependency tree

...

Do you want to continue? [Y/n] Y

...
```

If you want to uninstall a package and all its dependencies, use the apt-get autoremove command:

```
jamal@jamal-VirtualBox:~$ sudo apt-get autoremove filezilla

Reading package lists... Done

...

The following packages will be REMOVED:

  filezilla filezilla-common libfilezilla0 libpugixml1v5 lib-
wxbase3.0-0v5 libwxgtk3.0-0v5

...

Do you want to continue? [Y/n] Y

...
```

ps

The ps command on Linux is one of the most basic commands for viewing processes running on the system. It provides a snapshot of the current processes along with detailed information like user id, cpu usage, memory usage, command name etc.

When ps is used without any options, it sends to standard output, four items of information for at least two processes currently on the system:

```
jamal@jamal-VirtualBox:~$ ps
```

```
 PID TTY           TIME CMD

 2294 pts/2     00:00:00 bash

 2412 pts/2     00:00:00 ps
```

PID is the process ID, it is very important.

CMD is the name of the command that launched the process.

To obtain much more complete information about the processes currently on the system, use the following command:

```
jamal@jamal-VirtualBox:~$ ps -aux | less

USER        PID %CPU %MEM    VSZ    RSS TTY      STAT START    TIME COMMAND

root          1  0.8  0.3  24944   5004 ?        Ss   14:27    0:14 /sbin/init
splash

root          2  0.0  0.0      0      0 ?        S    14:27    0:00 [kthreadd]

root          4  0.0  0.0      0      0 ?        S<   14:27    0:00 [kworker/0:0H]

...
```

The -a option tells ps to list the processes of all users on the system.

The -u option is used to provide detailed information about each process.

The -x option adds to the list, processes that have no controlling terminal, such as daemons, which are programs that are launched during booting (i.e., computer start-up) and run unobtrusively in the background until they are activated by a particular event or condition.

To sort processes by cpu or memory usage, do it like this:

```
jamal@jamal-VirtualBox:~$ ps -aux --sort=-pcpu,+pmem | head -5

USER        PID %CPU %MEM    VSZ    RSS TTY      STAT START    TIME COMMAND

jamal      1512  9.9  8.2 294740 126456 ?        Ssl  14:30    3:53 compiz

root          6  1.3  0.0      0      0 ?        S    14:27    0:33 [ksoftirqd/0]

...
```

To display processes by process id, use the "-p" option and provide the process id (or ids separated by comma):

```
jamal@jamal-VirtualBox:~$ ps -up 1512
```

USER	PID	%CPU	%MEM	VSZ	RSS	TTY	STAT	START	TIME	COMMAND
jamal	1512	8.3	8.0	291932	123752	?	Ssl	14:30	3:57	compiz

Let's create a shell script and monitor its execution using the ps command, use these commands to set up and run the shell script: (Notice the script process ID **2986**)

```
jamal@jamal-VirtualBox:~$ echo '#!/bin/bash

> for i in {1..20}

> do

> sleep 1

> done' > shell-script.sh


jamal@jamal-VirtualBox:~$ chmod 755 shell-script.sh


jamal@jamal-VirtualBox:~$ ./shell-script.sh &
[1] 2986
```

You can monitor the execution with ps like this:

```
jamal@jamal-VirtualBox:~$ ps -p 2986

 PID TTY          TIME CMD

 2986 pts/2    00:00:00 shell-script.sh
```

The output tells you that the script is always running, wait a little time and retry to see if it's done:

```
jamal@jamal-VirtualBox:~$ ps -p 2986

 PID TTY          TIME CMD
[1]+  Done                    ./shell-script.sh
```

Likewise, each command that runs as a background job (e.g. gzip) can be monitored by the ps command.

du

The du (Disk Usage) command is used to check the information of disk usage of files and directories.

For example, use it this way to find out the disk usage summary of the /home directory tree and each of its subdirectories:

```
jamal@jamal-VirtualBox:~$ du -h /home | less

32K      /home/kevin

4.0K     /home/jamal/.local/share/unity-settings-daemon

4.0K     /home/jamal/.local/share/evolution/mail/trash

8.0K     /home/jamal/.local/share/evolution/mail

...
```

And to get simply the size of /home, use the -s or --summarize option that displays only a total for each argument:

```
jamal@jamal-VirtualBox:~$ du -sh /home

18M      /home
```

You can also use the '-c' option to get a grand total usage disk space at the last line:

```
jamal@jamal-VirtualBox:/$ du -ch /home/jamal

4.0K     /home/jamal/.local/share/unity-settings-daemon

4.0K     /home/jamal/.local/share/evolution/mail/trash

8.0K     /home/jamal/.local/share/evolution/mail

...

18M      total
```

chown

The owner of a file can be changed with the chown command; we'll exercise a scenario about ownership.

Firstly, use the su command to switch to root and create two users, bruce and jason:

```
jamal@jamal-VirtualBox:/$ su root

Password:
```

```
root@jamal-VirtualBox:/# useradd bruce

root@jamal-VirtualBox:/# useradd jason
```

After that, switch to bruce and create a file named bruce-notes.txt in the /tmp directory:

```
root@jamal-VirtualBox:/# su bruce

bruce@jamal-VirtualBox:/$ cd /tmp

bruce@jamal-VirtualBox:/tmp$ touch bruce-notes.txt
```

bruce and his primary group are the owners of this file, anyone else has just the read permission, and bruce can control this permission and **re- move** it from others as we do here:

```
bruce@jamal-VirtualBox:/tmp$ ls -l bruce-notes.txt
-rw-rw-r-- 1 bruce bruce 0 dec 14 00:37 bruce-notes.txt

bruce@jamal-VirtualBox:/tmp$ chmod o-r bruce-notes.txt
```

Now switch to root then to jason, try to access bruce file, you'll get a permission denied error message:

```
bruce@jamal-VirtualBox:/tmp$ su root
Password:

root@jamal-VirtualBox:/tmp# su jason

jason@jamal-VirtualBox:/tmp$ cat bruce-notes.txt
cat: bruce-notes.txt: Permission denied
```

Only the root admin can change the ownership and grant it to Jason, let's do it:

```
jason@jamal-VirtualBox:/tmp$ su root
```

```
Password:

root@jamal-VirtualBox:/tmp# chown jason:jason bruce-notes.txt

root@jamal-VirtualBox:/tmp# ls -l bruce-notes.txt
-rw-rw---- 1 jason jason 0 dec 14 00:37 bruce-notes.txt
```

Now, when bruce tries to access his file, he gets a permission denied because he is not the owner anymore, and because he has removed the read permission to other users when he was the owner:

```
root@jamal-VirtualBox:/tmp# su bruce

bruce@jamal-VirtualBox:/tmp$ cat bruce-notes.txt
cat: bruce-notes.txt: Permission denied
```

Jason as the owner can modify the file, rename it and even grant bruce the read permission:

```
bruce@jamal-VirtualBox:/tmp$ su root
Password:

root@jamal-VirtualBox:/tmp# su jason

jason@jamal-VirtualBox:/tmp$ mv bruce-notes.txt jason-notes.txt
jason@jamal-VirtualBox:/tmp$ chmod o+r jason-notes.txt

jason@jamal-VirtualBox:/tmp$ ls -l jason-notes.txt
-rw-rw-r-- 1 jason jason 0 dec 14 00:37 jason-notes.txt
```

19 MOUNTING

In Linux world, everything is a file. These files are organized in a tree structure, beginning at the root /.

Your file systems (disks, partitions, CD-ROM, remote directories) will then be mounted at the appropriate places in the root (/) according to the /etc/fstab file.

File system table

This file contains information about your file systems, which device they belong to and to which point they will get mounted. It is usually at /etc/fstab.

Below is an example of an fstab file:

# <file system>	<mount point>	<type>	<options>	<dump>	<pass>
/dev/hda3	/	ext3	defaults	1	1
/dev/hda4	/tmp	ext2	defaults	1	2
# removable disks					
/dev/cdrom	/mnt/cdrom	udf,iso9660	noauto,owner	0	0
/dev/fd0	/mnt/floppy	auto	noauto,owner	0	0
# A FAT partition that Linux and Windows can read and write					
/dev/hda5	/mnt/shared	vfat	umask=000	0	0

Here is the description of the most important columns:

File system: This field is the path to the device file or the label that describes the volume.

Mount point: specifies where to mount the device.

Type: specifies the device's file system type.

Options: specifies the additional options accepted when mounting the device. Options include options for permissions on the volume, and for how the file system is mounted (either automatically or specific users who can mount the file system). Options can be strung together in comma-separated list.

Mounting facts

When you mount a volume, you mount it to a directory. When you access that directory in the file system, you are actually accessing the volume mounted to that directory.

Device files are located in the /dev directory.

You should always mount volumes and other storage devices to empty directories. If you mount a volume to a directory that contains data, the mounted volume makes that data inaccessible.

The /mnt and /media directories (depending on your system configuration) are directories that contain **mount points** specifically for external storage devices (e.g. CD-ROM drive, floppy drives, USB drives...).

If you get a disk is busy error when unmounting a device, make sure your current working directory is not in that file system. Also, run the command lsof +f -- <mountpoint or device>. This will allow you to close the file or at worse kill the process that has the file open.

Mounting commands

Let's take a look at our fstab file:

```
jamal@jamal-VirtualBox:/$ cat /etc/fstab | grep -v '^#'
UUID=4342428c-b059-4095-9e07-b0054e4e0221 /     ext4  errors=remount-ro 0   1
UUID=f609b9ba-0586-4599-8d9d-b8f903a23783 none  swap  sw              0   0
```

It is not very helpful to understand the UUID of a drive partition, use this command to convert it to the familiar /dev device name:

```
jamal@jamal-VirtualBox:~$ grep '^UUID' /etc/fstab | while read
line; do findfs $( echo $line | cut -d' ' -f1 ); echo $line;done


/dev/sda1

UUID=8b9fe08d-70ad-41fc-b9e7-60f31c52050b / ext4 errors=remount-ro 0 1

/dev/sda5

UUID=2e36109c-4d9b-4f4f-b476-5c4f4a03e3a0 none swap sw 0 0
```

Note: as an exercise, try to analyse the command in the previous example (findfs allows to find a file system by label or UUID).

The output informs us that /dev/sda1 is mounted on the root (/). We can get much more information by using the mount command with no arguments:

```
jamal@jamal-VirtualBox:/$ mount

sysfs on /sys type sysfs (rw,nosuid,nodev,noexec,relatime)

proc on /proc type proc (rw,nosuid,nodev,noexec,relatime)

udev on /dev type devtmpfs (rw,nosuid,relatime,size=704768k,…

devpts on /dev/pts type devpts (rw,nosuid,noexec,relatime,gid=5,…

tmpfs on /run type tmpfs (rw,nosuid,noexec,relatime,size=…

/dev/sda1 on / type ext4 (rw,relatime,errors=remount-ro,data=ordered)

…
```

udev, tmpfs or sysfs file systems are advanced topics we won't discuss in this book, so to show only /dev mounted file systems type:

```
jamal@jamal-VirtualBox:~$ mount | grep '^/dev'
/dev/sda1 on / type ext4 (rw,relatime,errors=remount-ro,data=ordered)
```

Again, this simply means that the first SCSI drive (sda1) is mounted on the root /.

To exercise mounting commands, we'll look for the cdrom device in the /dev directory and mount it to /media/VBox_GAs_5.2.1:

```
jamal@jamal-VirtualBox:~$ pwd
/home/jamal
jamal@jamal-VirtualBox:~$ cd /dev

jamal@jamal-VirtualBox:/dev$ ls -l | grep -E '(cdrom|cd-rom)'
lrwxrwxrwx  1 root root            3 Dec 25 22:05 cdrom -> sr0
crw-rw----+ 1 root cdrom    21,     0 Dec 25 22:05 sg0
brw-rw----+ 1 root cdrom    11,     0 Dec 25 22:05 sr0
```

The name of the cdrom device is **sr0,** type the command below to un-mount the device if it's already mounted:

```
jamal@jamal-VirtualBox:~$ sudo umount /dev/sr0
```

Now let's create the mounting point, we're talking about /media/VBox_GAs_5.2.1:

```
jamal@jamal-VirtualBox:/dev$ cd /media
jamal@jamal-VirtualBox:/media$ ls -l
total 0

jamal@jamal-VirtualBox:/media$ sudo mkdir VBox_GAs_5.2.1
[sudo] password for jamal:
```

Then we use the mount command:

```
$ sudo mount -t iso9660 /dev/sr0 /media/VBox_GAs_5.2.1
mount: no medium found on /dev/sr0
```

An error message occurs; it indicates that no medium is found on /dev/sr0, we should insert a cdrom into our device to get the mount work. (If you've done it before you won't get this error, just skip this part)

On the virtual box, select the VM then click Settings:

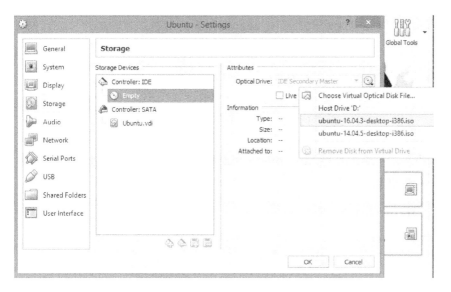

Click the cdrom button and add a medium (iso file) then Click Ok.

Try it again:

```
$ sudo mount -t iso9660 /dev/sr0 /media/VBox_GAs_5.2.1/
mount: /dev/sr0 is write-protected, mounting read-only
```

The -t option is used to indicate the given file system type.

The iso9660 argument describes standard and default file system structure to be used on CD/DVD ROMs.

To check the mounting, type:

```
jamal@jamal-VirtualBox:/$ mount | grep '^/dev'
/dev/sda1 on / type ext4 (rw,relatime,errors=remount-ro,data=ordered)
/dev/sr0 on /media/jamal/VBox_GAs_5.2.1 type iso9660 (ro,relatime)


jamal@jamal-VirtualBox:/$ ls /media/VBox_GAs_5.2.1/
32Bit  AUTORUN.INF  cert  runasroot.sh  VBoxLinuxAdditions.run
VBoxWindowsAdditions-amd64.exe  VBoxWindowsAdditions-x86.exe
64Bit  autorun.sh  OS2  TRANS.TBL    VBoxSolarisAdditions.pkg
VBoxWindowsAdditions.exe
```

To unmount the /dev/sr0 device, use the umount command:

```
jamal@jamal-VirtualBox:/$ sudo umount /dev/sr0


jamal@jamal-VirtualBox:/$ mount | grep '^/dev'
/dev/sda1 on / type ext4 (rw,relatime,errors=remount-ro,data=ordered)
```

df command

You can also use the df command to show which file systems are mounted to what points and to get information about the total usages:

```
jamal@jamal-VirtualBox:/$ df -hT

Filesystem       Type       Size  Used Avail Use% Mounted on

udev             devtmpfs   689M     0  689M   0% /dev

tmpfs            tmpfs      142M  4.7M  137M   4% /run

/dev/sda1        ext4       8.8G  4.2G  4.2G  51% /

tmpfs            tmpfs      708M  196K  708M   1% /dev/shm

tmpfs            tmpfs      5.0M  4.0K  5.0M   1% /run/lock

tmpfs            tmpfs      708M     0  708M   0% /sys/fs/cgroup

...
```

The h option (or --human-readable) transforms the output into a form understandable for common users.

The T option prints the file system type (the Type column).

df is useful specially to display the amount of disk space available on the file system **containing a specific file or directory**:

```
jamal@jamal-VirtualBox:~$ df -h /home

Filesystem       Size  Used Avail Use% Mounted on

/dev/sda1        8.8G  4.2G  4.2G  51% /
```

ENDING

At this point you should have a great knowledge in Linux commands and bash scripting, I hope so.

If you have a little time, let me know please your review, my email is jamalbayi@gmail.com.